Invent & Wander

Invent &
Wander

The Collected Writings of

JEFF
BEZOS

Harvard Business Review Press & PublicAffairs

Published by Harvard Business Review Press and PublicAffairs, an imprint of Perseus Books, LLC, a subsidiary of Hachette Book Group, Inc. The PublicAffairs name and logo is a trademark of the Hachette Book Group.

Printed in the United States of America

10 9 8 7 6 5 4 3 2 1

The web addresses referenced in this book were live and correct at the time of the book's publication but may be subject to change.

Editorial production by Christine Marra, Marrathon Production Services. www.marrathoneditorial.org

Book design by Jane Raese
Set in 10.5-point New Baskerville

Library of Congress Cataloging-in-Publication Data is forthcoming.

ISBN 978-1-64782-071-8 (hc), ISBN 978-1-64782-072-5 (e-book)

The paper used in this publication meets the requirements of the American National Standard for Permanence of Paper for Publications and Documents in Libraries and Archives Z39.48-1992.

HBR Press Quantity Sales Discounts

Harvard Business Review Press titles are available at significant quantity discounts when purchased in bulk for client gifts, sales promotions, and premiums. Special editions, including books with corporate logos, customized covers, and letters from the company or CEO printed in the front matter, as well as excerpts of existing books, can also be created in large quantities for special needs.

For details and discount information for both print and ebook formats, contact booksales@harvardbusiness.org, tel. 800-988-0886, or www.hbr.org/bulksales.

Contents

Part 1
The Shareholder Letters

Part 2
Life & Work

Invent & Wander

Introduction

by Walter Isaacson

I AM OFTEN ASKED who, of the people living today, I would consider to be in the same league as those I have written about as a biographer: Leonardo da Vinci, Benjamin Franklin, Ada Lovelace, Steve Jobs, and Albert Einstein. All were very smart. But that's not what made them special. Smart people are a dime a dozen and often don't amount to much. What counts is being creative and imaginative. That's what makes someone a true innovator. And that's why my answer to the question is Jeff Bezos.

So, what are the ingredients of creativity and imagination, and what makes me think that Bezos belongs in the same league as my other subjects?

The first is to be curious, passionately curious. Take Leonardo. In his delight-filled notebooks we see his mind dancing across all fields of nature with a curiosity that is exuberant and playful. He asks and tries to answer hundreds of charmingly random questions: Why is the sky blue? What does the tongue of a woodpecker look like? Do a bird's wings move faster when flapping up or when flapping down? How is the pattern of swirling water similar to that of curling hair? Is the muscle of the bottom lip connected to that of the top lip?

Leonardo did not need to know these things to paint the *Mona Lisa* (though it helped); he needed to know them because he was Leonardo, always obsessively curious. "I have no special talent," Einstein once said. "I am only passionately curious." That's not fully true (he certainly did have special talent), but he was right when he said, "Curiosity is more important than knowledge."

A second key trait is to love and to connect the arts and sciences. Whenever Steve Jobs launched a new product such as the iPod or iPhone, his presentation ended with street signs that showed an intersection of Liberal Arts Street and Technology Street. "It's in Apple's DNA that technology alone is not enough," he said at one of these presentations. "We believe that it's technology married with the humanities that yields us the result that makes our heart sing." Einstein, likewise, realized how important it is to interweave the arts and the sciences. When he felt stymied in his quest for the theory of general relativity, he would pull out his violin and play Mozart, saying that the music helped connect him to the harmony of the spheres. From Leonardo da Vinci, we have the greatest symbol of this connection between the arts and sciences: *Vitruvian Man,* his drawing of a nude male standing in a circle and a square, a triumph of anatomy, math, beauty, and spirituality.

In fact, it helps to be excited by all disciplines. Leonardo da Vinci and Benjamin Franklin wanted to know everything you could possibly know about everything that was knowable. They studied anatomy and botany and music and art and weaponry and water engineering and everything in between. People who love all fields of knowledge are the ones who can best spot the patterns that exist across nature. Both Franklin and Leonardo were fascinated by whirlwinds and swirling water. That helped Franklin figure out how storms move up the coast and to chart the Gulf Stream. It helped Leonardo understand how the heart valve works as well as to paint both the water rippling by the ankles of Jesus in the *Baptism of Christ* and the curls of the *Mona Lisa.*

Another characteristic of truly innovative and creative people is that they have a reality-distortion field, a phrase that was used about Steve Jobs and comes from a *Star Trek* episode in which aliens create an entire new world through sheer mental force. When his colleagues protested that one of Jobs's ideas or proposals would be impossible to implement, he would use a trick he learned from a guru in India: he would stare at them without blinking and say, "Don't be afraid. You can do it." It usually worked. He drove people mad, he drove them to distraction, but he also drove them to do things they didn't believe they could do.

Related to that is the ability to "think different," as Jobs put it in a memorable set of Apple ads. The science community at the beginning of the twentieth century was puzzling over how the speed of light seemed to remain constant no matter how fast the observer was moving toward or away from the source. At the time Albert Einstein was a third-class patent clerk in Switzerland who was studying devices that sent signals between different clocks in order to synchronize them. He came up with an out-of-the-box thought based on his realization that people who were in different states of motion would have different perceptions of whether the clocks were synchronized. Perhaps the speed of light is always constant, he theorized, because time itself is relative depending on one's state of motion. It took the rest of the physics community a few years to realize that this "theory of relativity" was right.

One final trait shared by all my subjects is that they retained a childlike sense of wonder. At a certain point in life most of us quit puzzling over everyday phenomena. Our teachers and parents, becoming impatient, tell us to stop asking so many silly questions. We might savor the beauty of a blue sky, but we no longer bother to wonder why it is that color. Leonardo did. So did Einstein, who wrote to another friend, "You and I never cease to stand like curious children before the great mystery into which we were born." We should be careful to never outgrow our wonder years—or to let our children do so.

Jeff Bezos embodies these traits. He has never outgrown his wonder years. He retains an insatiable, childlike, and joyful curiosity about almost everything. His interest in narrative and storytelling not only comes from Amazon's roots in the bookselling business; it is also a personal passion. As a kid, Bezos read dozens of science fiction novels each summer at a local library, and he now hosts an annual retreat for writers and moviemakers. Likewise, although his interest in robotics and artificial intelligence was sparked because of Amazon, these fields have grown to become intellectual passions, and he now hosts another gathering each year that brings together experts interested in machine learning, automation, robotics, and space. He collects historical artifacts from great moments in science, exploration, and discovery. And he connects this love of the humanities and his passion for technology to his instinct for business.

That trifecta—humanities, technology, business—is what has made him one of our era's most successful and influential innovators. Like Steve Jobs, Bezos has transformed multiple industries. Amazon, the world's largest online retailer, has changed how we shop and what we expect of shipping and deliveries. More than half of US households are members of Amazon Prime, and Amazon delivered ten billion packages in 2018, which is two billion more than the number of people on this planet. Amazon Web Services (AWS) provides cloud computing services and applications that enable start-ups and established companies to easily create new products and services, just as the iPhone App Store opened whole new pathways for business. Amazon's Echo has created a new market for smart home speakers, and Amazon Studios is making hit TV shows and movies. Amazon is also poised to disrupt the health and pharmacy industries. At first its purchase of the Whole Foods Market chain was confounding, until it became apparent that the move could be a brilliant way to tie together the strands of a new Bezos business model, which involves retailing, online ordering, and superfast delivery, combined with physical outposts. Bezos is also building a private space company with the long-term goal of moving heavy industry to space, and he has become the owner of the *Washington Post*.

Of course, he also has some of the infuriating traits that distinguished Steve Jobs and others. Despite his fame and influence, he has remained, behind his boisterous laugh, somewhat of an enigma. But through his life tale and writings, it is possible to get a sense of what drives him.

When Jeff Bezos was a young kid—big eared, with a booming laugh and insatiable curiosity—he spent his summers on the sprawling South Texas ranch of his maternal grandfather, Lawrence Gise, an upright but loving naval commander who had helped develop the hydrogen bomb as an assistant director of the Atomic Energy Commission. There Jeff learned self-reliance. When a bulldozer broke, he and his grandfather built a crane to lift out the gears and fix them. Together they castrated the cattle, built windmills, laid pipe, and had long conversations about the frontiers of science, technology, and space travel. "He did all his own veterinary work," Bezos recalls. "He would make his own needles to suture up the cattle with. He would take a piece of wire, use a blowtorch to heat it up, pound it flat, sharpen it, drill a hole through it—make a needle. Some of the cattle even survived."

Jeff was a voracious reader with an adventurous mind. His grandfather would take him to the library, which had a huge collection of science fiction books. Over the summers Jeff worked his way through the shelves, reading hundreds of them. Isaac Asimov and Robert Heinlein became his favorites, and later in life he would not only quote them but also occasionally invoke their rules, lessons, and lingo.

His self-reliance and adventurous spirit were also instilled by Jeff's mother, Jackie, who was just as tenacious and sharp as her father and son. She became pregnant with Jeff when she was only seventeen. "She was a high school student," Jeff explains. "You're probably thinking, 'Wow in 1964 in Albuquerque, it was probably really cool to be a pregnant girl.' No, it wasn't. It took a lot of grit. And a lot of help from her parents. The high school actually even tried to kick her out of school. I guess they thought pregnancy might be contagious. And my grandfather being a cool and wise guy negotiated a deal with the principal that allowed her to stay and finish high school." What was the main lesson Jeff learned from her? "You grow up with a mother like that and you have unbelievable grit," he says.

Jeff's biological father ran a bicycle store and performed in a circus unicycle troupe. He and Jackie were married only briefly. When Jeff was four, his mother remarried. Her second husband was a better match, a person who also taught Jeff the value of grit and determination: Miguel Bezos, known as Mike. He, too, was self-reliant and adventurous. He had come to the United States at age sixteen as a refugee from Fidel Castro's Cuba, traveling on his own and wearing a jacket his mother had sewed for him out of household rags. After he married Jackie, he adopted her lively son, who took his last name and forever after considered him his real father.

As a five-year-old in July 1969, Jeff watched television coverage of the Apollo 11 mission that culminated with Neil Armstrong walking on the moon. It was a seminal moment. "I remember watching it on our living room TV, and the excitement of my parents and my grandparents," he says. "Little kids can pick up that kind of excitement. They know something extraordinary is happening. That definitely became a passion of mine." Among other things, his exhilaration about space turned him into one of those hard-core *Star Trek* fans who knows every episode.

At his Montessori preschool Bezos was already fanatically focused. "The teacher complained to my mother that I was too task focused and that she couldn't get me to switch tasks, so she would have to just pick up my chair and move me," he recalls. "And by the way, if you ask the people who work with me, that's still probably true today."

In 1974, when he was ten, his passion for *Star Trek* led him to computers. He discovered that he could play a space video game on the terminal in the computer room of his elementary school in Houston, where his father was working for Exxon. This was in the days before personal computers, and a dial-up modem connected the school's computer terminal to the mainframe of a company that had donated its excess computer time. "We had a teletype that was connected by an old acoustic modem," Bezos says. "You literally dialed a regular phone and picked up the handset and put it in this little cradle. And nobody—none of the teachers knew how to operate this computer, nobody did. But there was a stack of manuals, and me and a couple of other kids stayed after class and learned how to program this thing. . . . And then, we learned that the mainframe programmers in some central location somewhere in Houston had already programmed this computer to play *Star Trek*. And from that day forward all we did was play *Star Trek*."

His mother encouraged his love of electronics and mechanics by shuttling him to and from RadioShack and letting him turn the family garage into a science project lab. She even indulged his penchant for creating ingenious booby traps to frighten his younger brother and sister. "I was constantly booby-trapping the house with various kinds of alarms and some of them were not just audible sounds, but actually like physical booby traps," he says. "My mom is a saint, because she would drive me to RadioShack multiple times a day."

His childhood business heroes were Thomas Edison and Walt Disney. "I've always been interested in inventors and invention," he says. Even though Edison was the more prolific inventor, Bezos came to admire Disney more because of the audacity of his vision. "It seemed to me that he had this incredible capability to create a vision that he could get a large number of people to share," he says. "Things that Disney invented, like Disneyland, the theme parks, they were such big visions that no single individual could ever pull them off, unlike a lot of the things that Edison worked on. Walt Disney really was able to get a big team of people working in a concerted direction."

By the time he was in high school, his family had moved to Miami. Bezos was a straight-A student, somewhat nerdy, and still completely obsessed with space exploration. He was chosen as the valedictorian of his class, and his speech was about space: how to colonize planets, build space hotels, and save our fragile planet by finding other places to do manufacturing. "Space, the final frontier, meet me there!" he concluded.

He went to Princeton with the goal of studying physics. It sounded like a smart plan until he smashed into a course on quantum mechanics. One day he and his roommate were trying to solve a particularly difficult partial differential equation, and they went to the room of another person in the class for help. He stared at it for a moment, then gave them the answer. Bezos was amazed that the student had done the calculation—which took three pages of detailed algebra to explain—in his head. "That was the very moment when I realized I was never going to be a great theoretical physicist," Bezos says. "I saw the writing on the wall, and I changed my major very quickly to electrical engineering and computer science." It was a difficult realization. His heart had been set on becoming a physicist, but finally he had confronted his own limits.

After graduation Bezos went to New York to apply his computer skills to the financial industry. He ended up at a hedge fund run by David E. Shaw, which used computer algorithms to discover pricing disparities in the financial markets. Bezos took to the work with a disciplined zeal. Foreshadowing the workplace fanaticism he would later try to instill at Amazon, he kept a sleeping bag in his office in case he wanted to sleep there after a late night of work.

While working at the hedge fund in 1994, Bezos came across the statistic that the web had been growing by more than 2,300 percent each year. He decided that he wanted to get aboard that rocket, and he came up with the idea of opening a retail store online, sort of a Sears catalogue for the digital age. Realizing that it was prudent to start with one product, he chose books—partly because he liked them and also because they were not perishable, were a commodity, and could be bought from two big wholesale distributors. And there were more than three million titles in print—far more than a bricks-and-mortar store could possibly keep on display.

When he told David Shaw that he wanted to leave the hedge fund to pursue this idea, Shaw took him on a two-hour walk through Central Park. "You know what, Jeff, this is a really good idea. I think you're onto a good idea here but this would be a better idea for somebody who didn't already have a good job." He convinced Bezos to think about it for a couple of days before making a decision. Bezos then consulted his wife, MacKenzie, whom he had met at the hedge fund and married the year before. "You know you can count me in 100 percent, whatever you want to do," she said.

To make the decision, Bezos used a mental exercise that would become a famous part of his risk-calculation process. He called it a "regret minimization framework." He would imagine what he would feel when he turned eighty and thought back to the decision. "I want to have minimized the number of regrets I have," he explains. "I knew that when I was eighty, I was not going to regret having tried this. I was not going to regret trying to participate in this thing called the internet that I thought was going to be a really big deal. I knew that if I failed, I wouldn't regret that, but I knew the one thing I might regret is not ever having tried. I knew that that would haunt me every day."

He and MacKenzie flew to Texas, where they borrowed a Chevrolet from Jeff's father and began a drive that would become legendary in entrepreneurial origin tales. As MacKenzie drove, Jeff typed up a business plan and spreadsheets filled with revenue predictions. "You know the business plan won't survive its first encounters with reality," he says. "But the discipline of writing the plan forces you to think through some of the issues and to get sort of mentally comfortable in the space. Then you start to understand, if you push on this knob, this will move over here and so on. So, that's the first step."

Bezos picked Seattle as a location for his new company, partly because it was home to Microsoft and many other tech companies and therefore had a lot of engineers to recruit from. It was also near a book distribution company. Bezos wanted to incorporate right away, so on the drive he called a friend to get a recommendation for a lawyer in Seattle. It turned out to be the friend's divorce lawyer, but he was able to handle the papers. Bezos told the lawyer he wanted to call the new company Cadabra, as in the magical incantation "abracadabra." The lawyer responded, "Cadaver?" Bezos unleashed his trademark boom of a laugh and realized he would need to come up with a better name. He eventually decided to name what he hoped would be the Earth's largest store after the Earth's longest river.

When he called his father to tell him what he was doing, Mike Bezos asked, "What's the Internet?" Or at least that's Jeff's romantic narrative. Mike Bezos in fact had been a user of the early online dial-up services and had a pretty good idea of what online retailing could be. Even though he and Jackie thought it was rash to leave a high-paying financial industry job for such a lark, they took much of their life savings—$100,000 at first, then more—and agreed to invest. "The initial start-up capital came primarily from my parents, and they invested a large fraction of their life savings in what became Amazon.com," Bezos says. "That was a very bold and trusting thing for them to do."

Mike Bezos admitted that he never understood either the concept or the business plan. "He was making a bet on his son, as was my mother," Jeff says. "I told them that I thought there was a 70 percent chance that they would lose their whole investment. . . . I thought I was giving myself triple the normal odds, because really, if you look at the odds of a start-up company succeeding at all, it's only about 10 percent. Here I was, giving myself a 30 percent chance." As his mother, Jackie, later said, "We didn't invest in Amazon, we invested in Jeff." They eventually put in more money, ended up owning 6 percent of the company, and used their wealth to become very active and creative philanthropists focused on providing early-childhood learning opportunities for all children.

Others didn't quite get the idea either. Craig Stoltz was then a *Washington Post* reporter running the newspaper's magazine about consumer technology. Bezos came to pitch his idea. "He was short, with an uncomfortable smile, thinning hair, and a somehow febrile affect," Stoltz later wrote in a blog post. Totally unimpressed, Stoltz blew him off and declined to write a story about the idea. Years later, long after Stoltz left the paper, Bezos would end up buying it.

Jeff and MacKenzie initially set up the company in the two-bedroom home they rented near Seattle. "They converted the garage into a work space and brought in three Sun workstations," Josh Quittner later wrote in *Time.* "Extension cords snaked from every available outlet in the house to the garage, and a black hole gaped through the ceiling—this was where a potbellied stove had been ripped out to make more room. To save money, Bezos went to Home Depot and bought three wooden doors. Using angle brackets and 2-by-4s, he hammered together three desks, at a cost of $60 each."

Amazon.com went live on July 16, 1995. Bezos and his small team rigged up a bell to chime whenever they got a sale, but it very quickly needed to be disabled, as rushes of orders came in. In the first month, with no real marketing or publicity plan other than asking friends to spread the word, Amazon scored sales in all fifty states and in forty-five countries. "Within the first few days, I knew this was going to be huge," Bezos told *Time.* "It was obvious that we were onto something much bigger than we ever dared to hope."

At first Jeff and MacKenzie and a few early employees handled everything, including packing, wrapping, and driving the boxes off to be shipped. "We had so many orders that we weren't ready for that we had no real organization in our distribution center at all," Bezos says. "In fact, we were packing on our hands and knees on a hard concrete floor." One of the other iconic origin tales of Amazon, told often by Bezos with his raucous laugh, involved how they figured out a way to make the packing easier.

"This packing is killing me! My back hurts, this is killing my knees on this hard cement floor," Bezos exclaimed one day. "You know what we need? We need knee pads!"

An employee looked at Bezos as if he were the stupidest person he'd ever seen. "What we need are packing tables," he said.

Bezos looked at the employee as if he were a genius. "I thought that was the smartest idea I had ever heard," Bezos recalls. "The next day we got packing tables, and I think we doubled our productivity."

The fact that Amazon grew so quickly meant that Bezos and his colleagues were unprepared for many of the challenges. But he sees a silver lining in the way they had to hustle. "It formed a culture of customer service in every department of the company," he says. "Every single person in the company, because we had to work with our hands so close to the customers, making sure those orders went out, really set up a culture that served us well, and that is our goal, to be Earth's most customer-centric company."

Bezos's goal soon became to create an "everything store." His next steps were to branch out to music and videos. Keeping his focus on the customer, he emailed one thousand of them to see what else they would like to be able to buy. The answers helped him understand better the concept of "the long tail," which means being able to offer items that are not everyday bestsellers and, thus, don't command shelf space at most retailers. "The way they answered the question was with whatever they were looking for at that moment," he says. "I remember one of the answers was 'I wish you sold windshield wiper blades because I really need windshield wiper blades.' And I thought to myself we can sell anything this way, and then we launched electronics and toys and many other categories over time."

At the end of 1999 I was the editor of *Time*, and we made a somewhat offbeat decision to make Bezos our Person of the Year, even though he wasn't a famous world leader or statesman. I had the theory that the people who affect our lives the most are often the people in business and technology who, at least early in their careers, aren't often found on the front pages. For example, we had made Andy Grove of Intel the Person of the Year at the end of 1997 because I felt the explosion of the microchip was changing our society more than any prime minister or president or treasury secretary.

But as the publication date of our Bezos issue neared in December 1999, the air was starting to go out of the dot.com bubble. I was worried—correctly—that internet stocks, such as Amazon, would start to collapse. So I asked the CEO of Time Inc., the very wise Don Logan, whether I was making a mistake by choosing Bezos and would look silly in years to come if the internet economy deflated. No, Don told me. "Stick with your choice. Jeff Bezos is not in the internet business. He's in the customer-service business. He will be around for decades to come, well after people have forgotten all the dot. coms that are going to go bust."

So we went ahead. The great portrait photographer Greg Heisler convinced Bezos to pose with his head facing out from an Amazon box filled with packaging material, and at the house of Margaret Carlson we threw a party featuring only food and drink that had been ordered online. Joshua Cooper Ramo, one of our savviest young editors, wrote the overview story that put Bezos in historical perspective:

> Every time a seismic shift takes place in our economy, there are people who feel the vibrations long before the rest of us do, vibrations so strong they demand action—action that can seem rash, even stupid. Ferry owner Cornelius Vanderbilt jumped ship when he saw the railroads coming. Thomas Watson Jr., overwhelmed by his sense that computers would be everywhere even when they were nowhere, bet his father's office-machine company on it: IBM. Jeffrey Preston Bezos had that same experience when he first peered into the maze of connected computers called the World Wide Web and realized that the future of retailing was glowing back at him. . . . Bezos' vision of the online

retailing universe was so complete, his Amazon.com site so elegant and appealing, that it became from Day One the point of reference for anyone who had anything to sell online. And that, it turns out, is everyone.

Amazon was indeed hit hard by the internet-bubble collapse. Its stock was at $106 a share in December 1999 when our Person of the Year issue came out. A month later it was down 40 percent. Within two years it had fallen to as low as $6 a share. Journalists and stock analysts ridiculed it, dubbing the company "Amazon.toast" and "Amazon.bomb." In the annual shareholder letter he wrote right after that, Bezos began with a one-word sentence: "Ouch."

But Don Logan was right. Amazon and Bezos were able to survive the bust. "As I watched the stock fall from 113 to 6, I was also watching all of our internal business metrics: number of customers, profit per unit," he says. "Every single thing about the business was getting better and fast. It's a fixed-cost business. And so, what I could see is that, from the internal metrics, is that at a certain volume level that we would cover our fixed costs and the company would be profitable."

Bezos succeeded by keeping his eye on the long game, foregoing profits for growth, and being relentless and sometimes ruthless with competitors and even his own colleagues. At one point during the dot.com meltdown, he and a few other internet entrepreneurs were on an *NBC Nightly News* special with Tom Brokaw. "Mr. Bezos, can you even spell 'profit'?" Brokaw asked, highlighting the fact that Amazon was hemorrhaging money as it grew. "Sure," Bezos replied, "P-R-O-P-H-E-T." And by 2019 Amazon stock would be at $2,000 a share, and the company would have $233 billion in revenues and 647,000 employees worldwide.

An example of how Bezos innovates and operates was the launch of Amazon Prime, which transformed the way Americans think about how quickly and cheaply they can be gratified by ordering online. One of his board members had been suggesting that Amazon create a loyalty program, similar to what the airlines have with their frequent-flyer programs. Separately, an Amazon engineer suggested that the company offer free shipping to its most loyal customers. Bezos put the two ideas together and asked his finance team to assess the costs and benefits. "The results were horrifying," Bezos says with his laugh. But Bezos had a rule, which was to use his heart and his intuition as well as empirical data in making a big decision. "There has to be risk taking. You have to have instinct. All the good decisions have to be made that way," he says. "You do it with a group. You do it with great humility."

He knew that creating Amazon Prime was what he calls a one-way door: it was a decision difficult to reverse. "We've made mistakes, doozies like the Fire Phone and many other things that just didn't work out. I won't list all of our failed experiments, but the big winners pay for thousands of failed experiments." He was aware that it would be scary at first because those who signed up for Prime would be the heaviest users of shipping. "What happens when you offer a free all-you-can-eat buffet, who shows up to the buffet first?" he says. "The heavy eaters. It's scary. It's, like, oh, my God, did I really say as many prawns as you can eat?" But eventually Amazon Prime led to the combination of a loyalty program and a convenience for customers as well as a huge source of customer data.

The greatest and most serendipitous innovation Bezos made was the creation of Amazon Web Services. The initial ideas—which included a software layer known as Elastic Compute Cloud and a hosting operation known as Simple Storage Service—bubbled up from inside the company. Eventually a variety of related ideas came together in a memo that proposed the creation of a service that would "enable developers and companies to use Web Services to build sophisticated and scalable applications."

Bezos seized on its potential and, sometimes with great passion erupting into bouts of fury, pushed his team to develop it faster and bigger. The result would supercharge internet entrepreneurship like no other platform since the iPhone App Store. It would enable any kid in a dorm room or any business on any Main Street—or any big corporation, for that matter—to experiment with ideas and build new services without having to buy racks of servers and suites of software. Instead, they could share in a globally distributed infrastructure of server farms, on-demand computing power, and applications that were more extensive than those of any company in the world.

"We completely reinvented the way that companies buy computation," Bezos says. "Traditionally, if you were a company and needed computation, you would build a data center, and you'd fill that data center with servers, and you'd have to upgrade the operating systems of those servers and keep everything running, and so on. None of that added any value to what the business was doing. It was kind of price-of-admission, undifferentiated heavy lifting." Bezos realized that this process was also holding back various groups of innovators within Amazon itself. The company's applications developers had been in a constant struggle with the hardware teams, but Bezos made them develop some standard application programming interfaces (APIs) and access to computing resources. "As soon as we did that, it was immediately obvious that every company in the world was going to want this," he says.

For a while a miracle happened: for a few years no other companies got into the space as competitors. Bezos's vision was far ahead of everyone else's. "It was the greatest piece of business luck in the history of business, so far as I know," he says.

Sometimes a failure and a success go together. That is what happened with the flop of Amazon's Fire Phone and the success of the Amazon Echo, the company's smart speaker and home assistant device known as Alexa. "While the Fire Phone was a failure, we were able to take our learnings (as well as the developers') and accelerate our efforts building Echo and Alexa," Bezos wrote in his 2017 stockholder letter.

His enthusiasm for Echo grew out of his love of *Star Trek*. When playing *Star Trek* games with his friends as a kid, Bezos liked to play the role of the computer on the starship *Enterprise*. "The vision for

Echo and Alexa was inspired by the *Star Trek* computer," he wrote. "The idea also had origins in two other arenas where we'd been building and wandering for years: machine learning and the cloud. From Amazon's early days, machine learning was an essential part of our product recommendations, and AWS gave us a front-row seat to the capabilities of the cloud. After many years of development, Echo debuted in 2014, powered by Alexa, who lives in the AWS cloud." The result was a wonderful combination of smart speakers, a *Star Trek* chatty home computer, and an intelligent personal assistant.

The genesis of Amazon Echo was, in one way, like Steve Jobs's development of Apple iPod. It arose out of intuition rather than focus groups, and it was not in response to some obvious customer demand. "No customer was asking for Echo," Bezos says. "Market research doesn't help. If you had gone to a customer in 2013 and said, 'Would you like a black, always-on cylinder in your kitchen about the size of a Pringles can that you can talk to and ask questions, that also turns on your lights and plays music?' I guarantee you they'd have looked at you strangely and said 'No, thank you.'" In a sweet irony, Bezos was able to trounce Apple in creating such a home device and then make its components—voice recognition and machine learning—work better than competing devices from both Google and, later, Apple.

Eventually Bezos hopes to integrate the Amazon online store, Amazon Prime, Echo, and Amazon's customer data analytics with the Whole Foods Market grocery chain, which Amazon bought in 2017. Bezos says that his purchase of the company was partly due to his admiration for the outlook of its founder, John Mackey. When he meets with the founder or chief executive of a company that Amazon is thinking of buying, Bezos tries to assess whether he or she is in it merely to make money or because of a true passion for serving customers. "I'm always trying to figure out one thing first and foremost: Is that person a missionary or a mercenary?" Bezos says. "The mercenaries are trying to flip their stock. The missionaries love their product or their service and love their customers and are trying to build a great service. By the way, the great paradox here is that it's usually the missionaries who make more money." Mackey struck him as a missionary, and his passion infused the Whole Foods ethos. "It's a missionary company, and he's a missionary guy."

Outside Amazon, Bezos's greatest enthusiasm, one nurtured since childhood, is space travel. In 2000 he set up a company, very secretively, near Seattle called Blue Origin, naming it after the pale blue planet where humans originated. He called upon one of his favorite science fiction writers, Neal Stephenson, to be an advisor. They kicked around wildly novel ideas, such as using a bullwhip-like device to propel objects into space. Eventually Bezos focused on reusable rockets. "How is the situation in the year 2000 different from 1960?" he asked. "The engines can be somewhat better, but they're still chemical rocket engines. What's different is computer sensors, cameras, software. Being able to land vertically is the kind of problem that can be addressed by those technologies that existed in 2000 that didn't exist in 1960."

In March 2003 Bezos began putting together a huge tract of ranchland in Texas where he could build his reusable rockets in secret. One of the great scenes in Christian Davenport's *The Space Barons* is the description of the helicopter trip Bezos took to find the land, which ended with a terrifying crash.

When reporter and Bezos biographer Brad Stone discovered the existence of Blue Origin, he emailed Bezos, asking for comment. Bezos wasn't ready to talk about it, but he did go on the record to push back against Stone's notion that he had founded the company because he thought that the government-run NASA program had become too risk averse and sluggish. "NASA is a national treasure, and it's total bull that anyone should be frustrated by NASA," Bezos wrote Stone. "The only reason I'm interested in space is because [NASA] inspired me when I was five years old. How many government agencies can you think of that inspire five-year-olds? The work NASA does is technically super-demanding and inherently risky, and they continue to do an outstanding job. The ONLY reason any of these small space companies have a chance of doing ANYTHING is because they get to stand on the shoulders of NASA's accomplishments and ingenuity."

Bezos approaches his space endeavors as a missionary rather than a mercenary. "This is the most important work I'm doing, and I have great conviction about that," he says. Earth is finite, and energy usage has grown so much that it will soon, he thinks, strain the resources of our small planet. That will leave us with a choice: accept static growth for humanity or explore and expand to places beyond Earth. "I want my grandchildren's grandchildren to be using way more energy per capita than I am," he says. "And I would like to see us not have a population cap. I wish there were a trillion humans in the solar system; then there would be a thousand Einsteins and a thousand Mozarts." But within a century, he fears, the Earth will not be able to sustain this growth of population and energy use. "So, what will that lead to? It will lead to stasis. I don't even think stasis is compatible with liberty." That prompted him to believe we should now begin thinking about new frontiers. "We can fix that problem," he says, by lowering the cost of access to space and using in-space resources.

Blue Origin is focused on lowering the cost of accessing space through its reusable launch vehicles and engines. *New Shepard*, named after the first American in space, Alan Shepard, was the first rocket to take off vertically, go to space, then land vertically back on Earth—and then it was the first to be reused again. Launching out of West Texas, *New Shepard* was designed from the beginning for human spaceflight and the rocket is getting ready to fly paying customers to space and back and has been launching research experiments on board for universities, research labs, and NASA. Blue Origin's larger orbital rocket, *New Glenn*, named after John Glenn, the first person to orbit the Earth, is poised to take commercial, NASA, and national security customers to space. In 2019 Bezos also announced the *Blue Moon* lunar lander, which was awarded a nearly $500 million contract from NASA to develop a system to take humans back to the moon. Blue Origin has partnered with Lockheed Martin, Northrop

Grumman, and Draper on the project. Separately, Bezos funded an expedition that recovered several of the F-1 engines that powered the *Saturn V* rocket to the moon during the Apollo program.

Another personal passion is the *Washington Post*, which Bezos bought in 2013. In an era when newspapers were declining, he infused the *Post* with cash, energy, technological skills, and new reporters while allowing its great editor, Martin Baron, unfettered editorial control. "I was not looking for a newspaper," Bezos says. "It had never occurred to me. It wasn't like a childhood dream." But then the paper's owner, Donald Graham, approached him and, over a series of conversations, convinced him that the mission was important. So Bezos did some soul searching and, as always, relied on intuition as well as analysis. "This is an important institution," he says he concluded. "This is the newspaper in the capital city of the most important country in the world. The *Washington Post* has an incredibly important role to play in this democracy." So he told Graham he would buy it, and he didn't haggle over the price. "I didn't negotiate with him and I did no due diligence," he says. "I wouldn't need to with Don. He told me every wart and pimple and he told me all the things that were great. And every single thing he told me on both sides of that ledger turned out to be true."

Although Bezos has made the paper better and more financially viable, the purchase has been very costly. Donald Trump neither understood nor cared that Bezos exercised no editorial control and that the paper was completely separate from Amazon. So the president, in ways that seem to me to be corrupt, has abused the power of the federal government to try to punish Amazon and deny contracts to Amazon Web Services that were merited.

Bezos's own politics and philosophy, which he does not impose on the *Post*, comprise a mix of social liberalism—he donated to the campaign to legalize gay marriage—and economic views that stress individual liberty. It is an attitude he shares with his father, who fled Castro's Cuba. "A free market economy, which by necessity involves a lot of liberty, just happens to work well in terms of allocating resources," he says. But the merit of the free market arises not merely from its efficiency but also from the moral value it accords to individuals, he believes.

> Imagine a world where some incredibly artificially intelligent computer could actually do a better job than the invisible hand of allocating resources, and were to say, "There shouldn't be this many chickens, there should be this many chickens," just a few more or a few less. Well, that might even lead to more aggregate wealth. So, it might be a society that if you give up liberty, everybody could be a little wealthier. Now, the question that I would pose is, if that turned out to be the world, "Is that a good trade?" Personally, I don't think so. Personally I think it would be a terrible trade. I think the American Dream is about liberty.

THROUGH THIS BOOK you can learn many of the lessons and secrets revealed in Bezos's interviews, writings, and the annual shareholder letters he has personally composed since 1997. Here are the five that I think are most important:

1. *Focus on the long term.* "*It's All About the Long Term,*" he said in the italicized initial headline in his first shareholder letter in 1997. "We will continue to make investment decisions in light of long-term market leadership considerations rather than short-term profitability considerations or short-term Wall Street reactions." Focusing on the long term allows the interests of your customers, who want better and faster services cheaper, and the interests of your shareholders, who want a return on investment, to come into alignment. That's not always true in the short term.

In addition, long-term thinking permits innovation. "We like to invent and do new things," he says, "and I know for sure that long-term orientation is essential for invention because you're going to have a lot of failures along the way."

Bezos's interest in space travel, he says, helps remind him to keep his focus on the distant horizon. Among his many strengths is his ability to keep his eye on that distant horizon, as he has done at Amazon. In the mission statement for his space company, he wrote, "Blue Origin will pursue this long-term objective patiently, step by step." As Elon Musk pushed his own competing space program forward with very public fits and starts, Bezos advised his team, "Be the tortoise and not the hare." Blue Origin's company shield has a Latin motto, *Gradatim Ferociter*: "Step by Step, Ferociously."

Among Bezos's many strengths is his ability to follow this motto by being exuberantly patient and patiently exuberant. At his Texas ranch Bezos has begun construction of a ten-thousand-year "clock of the long now," designed by the futurist Danny Hillis, which has a century hand that advances every hundred years and a cuckoo that comes out every millennium. "It's a special clock, designed to be a symbol, an icon for long-term thinking," he says.

2. *Focus relentlessly and passionately on the customer.* As he put it in his 1997 letter, "Obsess over Customers." Each annual letter reinforces that mantra. "We intend to build the world's most customer-centric company," he wrote the following year. "We hold as axiomatic that customers are perceptive and smart. . . . But there is no rest for the weary. I constantly remind our employees to be afraid, to wake up every morning terrified. Not of our competition, but of our customers."

In an interview with me at a conference sponsored by the Aspen Institute and *Vanity Fair*, Bezos elaborated. "The core of the company is customer obsession as opposed to competitor obsession," he said. "The advantage of being customer focused is that customers are always dissatisfied. They always want more, and so they pull you along. Whereas if you're competitor obsessed, if you're a leader, you can look around and you see everybody running behind you, maybe you slow down a little."

An example of keeping the focus on customers was his policy of allowing negative reviews of products to appear on Amazon. An investor complained that Bezos was forgetting that Amazon only makes money when it sells things, so negative reviews hurt the business. "When I read that letter, I thought, we don't make money when we sell things," Bezos says. "We make money when we help customers make purchase decisions."

Amazon gets criticized—as does Walmart—for squeezing suppliers and forcing them to cut costs. But Bezos sees "relentlessly lowering prices" for consumers as core to Amazon's mission. For most recent years Amazon has come in first in major surveys of customer satisfaction.

3. *Avoid PowerPoint and slide presentations.* This is a maxim that Steve Jobs also followed. Bezos's belief in the power of storytelling means that he thinks that his colleagues should be able to create a readable narrative when they pitch an idea. "We don't do PowerPoint (or any other slide-oriented) presentations at Amazon," he wrote in a recent shareholder letter. "Instead, we write narratively structured six-page memos. We silently read one at the beginning of each meeting in a kind of study hall."

The memos, which are limited to six pages, are supposed to be written with clarity, which Bezos believes (correctly) forces a clarity of thinking. They are often collaborative efforts, but they can have a personal style. Sometimes they incorporate proposed press releases. "Even in the example of writing a six-page memo, that's teamwork," he says. "Someone on the team needs to have the skill."

4. *Focus on the big decisions.* "As a senior executive, what do you really get paid to do?" he asks. "You get paid to make a small number of high-quality decisions. Your job is not to make thousands of decisions every day."

He divides the decisions that have to be made into those that can be walked back and those that are irrevocable. The latter require a lot more caution. In the case of the former, he tries to decentralize the process. At Amazon he created what he calls "multiple paths to yes." In other organizations, he points out, a proposal can be killed by supervisors at many levels, and it needs to pass through all those gates in order to be approved. At Amazon, employees can shop their ideas around to any of the hundreds of executives who are empowered to get to yes.

5. *Hire the right people.* "We will continue to focus on hiring and retaining versatile and talented employees," he wrote in an early shareholder letter. Compensation, especially early on, was heavily weighted to stock options rather than cash. "We know our success will be largely affected by our ability to attract and retain a motivated employee base, each of whom must think like, and therefore must actually be, an owner."

There are three criteria he instructs managers to consider when they are hiring: Will you admire this person? Will this person raise the average level of effectiveness of the group he or she is entering? Along what dimension might this person be a superstar?

It's never been easy to work at Amazon. When Bezos interviews people, he warns them, "You can work long, hard, or smart, but at Amazon.com you can't choose two out of three." Bezos makes no apologies. "We are working to build something important, something that matters to our customers, something that we can all tell our grandchildren about," he says. "Such things aren't meant to be easy. We are incredibly fortunate to have this group of dedicated employees whose sacrifices and passion build Amazon.com."

These lessons remind me of the way Steve Jobs operated. Sometimes such a style can be crushing, and to some people it may feel tough or even cruel. But it also can lead to the creation of grand, new innovations and companies that change the way we live.

Bezos has done all of this. But he still has many chapters to write in his story. He has always been public spirited, but I suspect in the coming years he will do more with philanthropy. Just as Bill Gates's parents led him into such endeavors, Jackie and Mike Bezos have been models for Bezos as he focuses on missions such as providing great early-childhood education to all kids.

I am also confident that he has at least one more major leap to make. I suspect that he will be—and is, indeed, eager to be—one of the first private citizens to blast himself into space. As he told his high school graduating class back in 1982, "Space, the final frontier, meet me there!"

FOR ALL THE YEARS of building Amazon to its formidable global role, Bezos could not have anticipated the cascade of crises in 2020. The COVID-19 pandemic created an immediate spike in demand for e-commerce deliveries as people were encouraged to stay home, and Amazon faced the daunting challenge of keeping its hundreds of thousands of warehouse workers safe. Bezos said his time and thinking were "wholly focused on COVID-19 and on how Amazon can best play its role." The *New York Times* reported that he was holding daily calls to help make decisions about issues such as inventory and virus testing, a marked change from recent years when Bezos had shifted day-to-day responsibilities to senior executives as he focused on long-term projects. And then there was the congressional pressure on the tech industry. On July 29, Bezos testified to a House hearing along with the CEOs of Facebook, Google, and Apple. In his testimony, Bezos framed the challenges the nation faced: "We're in the middle of a much-needed race reckoning. We also face the challenges of climate change and income inequality, and we're stumbling through the crisis of a global pandemic." And then he shifted his tone to the positivity of an entrepreneur. "Still, with all of our faults and problems, the rest of the world would love even the tiniest sip of the elixir we have here in the US . . . It's still Day One for this country."

A Note on Sourcing

All content in Part 1 and Part 2 of this book is drawn from the words and ideas of Jeff Bezos.

Part 1, "The Shareholder Letters," is composed of the letter sent by Jeff Bezos in April of each year to Amazon.com shareholders.

Part 2, "Life and Work," has been drawn from the following transcripts of interviews and speeches by Jeff Bezos:

Economic Club of Washington on September 13, 2018 (David Rubenstein interviewer)

The Climate Pledge Launch press conference on September 19, 2019

Washington Post Transformers conference on May 18, 2016

Jeff Bezos address to the Princeton graduating class of 2010

2019 Reagan National Defense Initiative (RNDF) conference, Ronald Reagan Institute (Fred Ryan presiding, Roger Zakheim interviewer) on December 7, 2019

Washington, DC, event on May 9, 2019, to unveil Blue Origin's lunar lander, *Blue Moon.*

Jeff Bezos's conversation with his brother, Mark Bezos, at Summit LA17 on November 4, 2017.

The sections of Part 2 are drawn from these sources as indicated:

My Gift in Life (Economic Club interview)
A Crucial Moment at Princeton (Economic Club interview)

Part 1

THE
SHAREHOLDER
LETTERS

It's All About the Long Term

1997

AMAZON.COM PASSED MANY milestones in 1997: by year-end, we had served more than 1.5 million customers, yielding 838 percent revenue growth to $147.8 million, and extended our market leadership despite aggressive competitive entry.

But this is Day 1 for the Internet and, if we execute well, for Amazon.com. Today, online commerce saves customers money and precious time. Tomorrow, through personalization, online commerce will accelerate the very process of discovery. Amazon.com uses the Internet to create real value for its customers and, by doing so, hopes to create an enduring franchise, even in established and large markets.

We have a window of opportunity as larger players marshal the resources to pursue the online opportunity and as customers, new to purchasing online, are receptive to forming new relationships. The competitive landscape has continued to evolve at a fast pace. Many large players have moved online with credible offerings and have devoted substantial energy and resources to building awareness, traffic, and sales. Our goal is to move quickly to solidify and extend our current position while we begin to pursue the online commerce opportunities in other areas. We see substantial opportunity in the large markets we are targeting. This strategy is not without risk: it requires serious investment and crisp execution against established franchise leaders.

It's All About the Long Term

We believe that a fundamental measure of our success will be the shareholder value we create over the *long term*. This value will be a direct result of our ability to extend and solidify our current market leadership position. The stronger our market leadership, the more powerful our economic model. Market leadership can translate directly to higher revenue, higher profitability, greater capital velocity, and correspondingly stronger returns on invested capital.

Our decisions have consistently reflected this focus. We first measure ourselves in terms of the metrics most indicative of our market leadership: customer and revenue growth, the degree to which our customers continue to purchase from us on a repeat basis, and the strength of our brand. We have invested and will continue to invest aggressively to expand and leverage our customer base, brand, and infrastructure as we move to establish an enduring franchise.

Because of our emphasis on the long term, we may make decisions and weigh trade-offs differently than some companies. Accordingly, we want to share with you our fundamental management and decision-making approach so that you, our shareholders, may confirm that it is consistent with your investment philosophy:

We will continue to focus relentlessly on our customers.

We will continue to make investment decisions in light of long-term market leadership considerations rather than short-term profitability considerations or short-term Wall Street reactions.

We will continue to measure our programs and the effectiveness of our investments analytically, to jettison those that do not provide acceptable returns, and to step up our investment in those that work best. We will continue to learn from both our successes and our failures.

We will make bold rather than timid investment decisions where we see a sufficient probability of gaining market leadership advantages. Some of these investments will pay off, others will not, and we will have learned another valuable lesson in either case.

When forced to choose between optimizing the appearance of our GAAP accounting and maximizing the present value of future cash flows, we'll take the cash flows.

We will share our strategic thought processes with you when we make bold choices (to the extent competitive pressures allow), so that you may evaluate for yourselves whether we are making rational long-term leadership investments.

We will work hard to spend wisely and maintain our lean culture. We understand the importance of continually reinforcing a cost-conscious culture, particularly in a business incurring net losses.

We will balance our focus on growth with emphasis on long-term profitability and capital management. At this stage, we choose to prioritize growth because we believe that scale is central to achieving the potential of our business model.

We will continue to focus on hiring and retaining versatile and talented employees and continue to weight their compensation to stock options rather than cash. We know our success will be largely affected by our ability to attract and retain a motivated employee base, each of whom must think like, and therefore must actually be, an owner.

We aren't so bold as to claim that the above is the "right" investment philosophy, but it's ours, and we would be remiss if we weren't clear in the approach we have taken and will continue to take.

With this foundation, we would like to turn to a review of our business focus, our progress in 1997, and our outlook for the future.

Obsess over Customers

From the beginning, our focus has been on offering our customers compelling value. We realized that the web was, and still is, the
World Wide Wait. Therefore, we set out to offer customers something they simply could not get any other way and began serving
them with books. We brought them much more selection than was
possible in a physical store (our store would now occupy six football fields), and presented it in a useful, easy-to-search, and easy-to-
browse format in a store open 365 days a year, twenty-four hours
a day. We maintained a dogged focus on improving the shopping
experience, and in 1997 substantially enhanced our store. We now
offer customers gift certificates, 1-Click^{SM} shopping, and vastly more
reviews, content, browsing options, and recommendation features.
We dramatically lowered prices, further increasing customer value.
Word of mouth remains the most powerful customer acquisition
tool we have, and we are grateful for the trust our customers have
placed in us. Repeat purchases and word of mouth have combined
to make Amazon.com the market leader in online bookselling.

By many measures, Amazon.com came a long way in 1997:

Sales grew from $15.7 million in 1996 to $147.8 million—an 838
percent increase.

Cumulative customer accounts grew from 180,000 to 1,510,000—a
738 percent increase.

The percentage of orders from repeat customers grew from over
46 percent in the fourth quarter of 1996 to over 58 percent in the
same period in 1997.

In terms of audience reach, per Media Metrix, our website went
from a rank of ninetieth to within the top twenty.

We established long-term relationships with many important
strategic partners, including America Online, Yahoo!, Excite, Net-
scape, GeoCities, AltaVista, @Home, and Prodigy.

Infrastructure

During 1997, we worked hard to expand our business infrastructure to support these greatly increased traffic, sales, and service levels:

Amazon.com's employee base grew from 158 to 614, and we significantly strengthened our management team.

Distribution center capacity grew from 50,000 to 285,000 square feet, including a 70 percent expansion of our Seattle facilities and the launch of our second distribution center in Delaware in November.

Inventories rose to over two hundred thousand titles at year-end, enabling us to improve availability for our customers.

Our cash and investment balances at year-end were $125 million, thanks to our initial public offering in May 1997 and our $75 million loan, affording us substantial strategic flexibility.

Our Employees

The past year's success is the product of a talented, smart, hardworking group, and I take great pride in being a part of this team. Setting the bar high in our approach to hiring has been, and will continue to be, the single most important element of Amazon .com's success.

It's not easy to work here (when I interview people I tell them, "You can work long, hard, or smart, but at Amazon.com you can't choose two out of three"), but we are working to build something important, something that matters to our customers, something that we can all tell our grandchildren about. Such things aren't meant to be easy. We are incredibly fortunate to have this group of dedicated employees whose sacrifices and passion build Amazon .com.

Goals for 1998

We are still in the early stages of learning how to bring new value to our customers through Internet commerce and merchandising. Our goal remains to continue to solidify and extend our brand and customer base. This requires sustained investment in systems and infrastructure to support outstanding customer convenience, selection, and service while we grow. We are planning to add music to our product offering, and over time we believe that other products may be prudent investments. We also believe there are significant opportunities to better serve our customers overseas, such as reducing delivery times and better tailoring the customer experience. To be certain, a big part of the challenge for us will lie not in finding new ways to expand our business, but in prioritizing our investments.

We now know vastly more about online commerce than when Amazon.com was founded, but we still have so much to learn. Though we are optimistic, we must remain vigilant and maintain a sense of urgency. The challenges and hurdles we will face to make our long-term vision for Amazon.com a reality are several: aggressive, capable, well-funded competition; considerable growth challenges and execution risk; the risks of product and geographic expansion; and the need for large continuing investments to meet an expanding market opportunity. However, as we've long said, online bookselling, and online commerce in general, should prove to be a very large market, and it's likely that a number of companies will see significant benefit. We feel good about what we've done, and even more excited about what we want to do.

1997 was indeed an incredible year. We at Amazon.com are grateful to our customers for their business and trust, to each other for our hard work, and to our shareholders for their support and encouragement.

Obsessions

1998

THE LAST THREE and a half years have been exciting. We've served a cumulative 6.2 million customers, exited 1998 with a $1 billion revenue run rate, launched music, video, and gift stores in the United States, opened shop in the United Kingdom and Germany, and, just recently, launched Amazon.com Auctions.

We predict the next three and a half years will be even more exciting. We are working to build a place where tens of millions of customers can come to find and discover anything they might want to buy online. It is truly Day 1 for the Internet and, if we execute our business plan well, it remains Day 1 for Amazon.com. Given what's happened, it may be difficult to conceive, but we think the opportunities and risks ahead of us are even greater than those behind us. We will have to make many conscious and deliberate choices, some of which will be bold and unconventional. Hopefully, some will turn out to be winners. Certainly, some will turn out to be mistakes.

Invent & Wander

A Recap of 1998

Heads-down focus on customers helped us make substantial progress in 1998:

Sales grew from $148 million in 1997 to $610 million—a 313 percent increase.

Cumulative customer accounts grew from 1.5 million at the end of 1997 to 6.2 million at the end of 1998—an increase of over 300 percent.

Despite this strong new customer growth, the percentage of orders placed on the Amazon.com website by repeat customers grew from over 58 percent in the fourth quarter of 1997 to over 64 percent in the same period in 1998.

Our first major product expansion, the Amazon.com music store, became the leading online music retailer in its first full quarter.

Following their October launch under the Amazon brand and with Amazon.com technology, the combined fourth-quarter sales in the UK and German stores nearly quadrupled over the third quarter, establishing Amazon.co.uk and Amazon.de as the leading online booksellers in their markets.

The addition of music was followed by the addition of video and gifts in November, and we became the leading online video retailer in only six weeks.

Twenty-five percent of our fourth-quarter 1998 sales was derived from Amazon.co.uk, Amazon.de, and music, video, and gift sales on Amazon.com, all very new businesses.

We significantly improved the customer experience, with innovations like 1-Click^{SM} shopping, Gift Click, storewide sales rank, and instant recommendations.

1998's revenue and customer growth and achievement of continued growth in 1999 were and are dependent on expansion of our infrastructure. Some highlights:

In 1998 our employee base grew from approximately six hundred to over twenty-one hundred, and we significantly strengthened our management team.

We opened distribution and customer service centers in the United Kingdom and Germany and in, early 1999, announced the lease of a highly mechanized distribution center of approximately 323,000 square feet in Fernley, Nevada. This latest addition will more than double our total distribution capacity and allows us to even further improve time-to-mailbox for customers.

Inventories rose from $9 million at the beginning of the year to $30 million by year end, enabling us to improve product availability for our customers and improve product costs through direct purchasing from manufacturers.

Our cash and investment balances, following our May 1998 high yield debt offering and early 1999 convertible debt offering, now stand at well over $1.5 billion (on a pro forma basis), affording us substantial financial strength and strategic flexibility.

We're fortunate to benefit from a business model that is cash-favored and capital efficient. As we do not need to build physical stores or stock those stores with inventory, our centralized distribution model has allowed us to build our business to a billion-dollar sales rate with just $30 million in inventory and $30 million in net plant and equipment. In 1998, we generated $31 million in operating cash flow which more than offset net fixed asset additions of $28 million.

Our Customers

We intend to build the world's most customer-centric company. We hold as axiomatic that customers are perceptive and smart, and that brand image follows reality and not the other way around. Our customers tell us that they choose Amazon.com and tell their friends about us because of the selection, ease-of-use, low prices, and service that we deliver.

But there is no rest for the weary. I constantly remind our employees to be afraid, to wake up every morning terrified. Not of our competition, but of our customers. Our customers have made our business what it is, they are the ones with whom we have a relationship, and they are the ones to whom we owe a great obligation. And we consider them to be loyal to us—right up until the second that someone else offers them a better service.

We must be committed to constant improvement, experimentation, and innovation in every initiative. We love to be pioneers, it's in the DNA of the company, and it's a good thing, too, because we'll need that pioneering spirit to succeed. We're proud of the differentiation we've built through constant innovation and relentless focus on customer experience, and we believe our initiatives in 1998 reflect it: our music, video, UK and German stores, like our US bookstore, are best of breed.

Work Hard, Have Fun, Make History

It would be impossible to produce results in an environment as dynamic as the Internet without extraordinary people. Working to create a little bit of history isn't supposed to be easy, and, well, we're finding that things are as they're supposed to be! We now have a team of twenty-one hundred smart, hard-working, passionate folks who put customers first. Setting the bar high in our approach to hiring has been, and will continue to be, the single most important element of Amazon.com's success.

During our hiring meetings, we ask people to consider three questions before making a decision:

Will you admire this person? If you think about the people you've admired in your life, they are probably people you've been able to learn from or take an example from. For myself, I've always tried hard to work only with people I admire, and I encourage folks here to be just as demanding. Life is definitely too short to do otherwise.

Will this person raise the average level of effectiveness of the group they're entering? We want to fight entropy. The bar has to continuously go up. I ask people to visualize the company five years from now. At that point, each of us should look around and say, "The standards are so high now—boy, I'm glad I got in when I did!"

Along what dimension might this person be a superstar? Many people have unique skills, interests, and perspectives that enrich the work environment for all of us. It's often something that's not even related to their jobs. One person here is a National Spelling Bee champion (1978, I believe). I suspect it doesn't help her in her everyday work, but it does make working here more fun if you can occasionally snag her in the hall with a quick challenge: "onomatopoeia!"

Goals for 1999

As we look forward, we believe that the overall e-commerce opportunity is enormous, and 1999 will be an important year. Although Amazon.com has established a strong leadership position, it is certain that competition will even further accelerate. We plan to invest aggressively to build the foundation for a multi-billion-dollar revenue company serving tens of millions of customers with operational excellence and high efficiency. Although this level of forward investment is costly and carries many inherent risks, we believe it will provide the best end-to-end experience for customers, and actually offer the least risky long-term value creation approach for investors.

The elements of our 1999 plan may not surprise you:

Distribution capacity: We intend to build out a significant distribution infrastructure to ensure that we can support all the sales our customers demand, with speedy access to a deep product inventory.

Systems capacity: We'll be expanding our systems capacity to support similar growth levels. The systems group has a significant task: expand to meet near term growth, restructure systems for multi-billion-dollar scale and tens of millions of customers, build out features and systems for new initiatives and new innovations, and increase operational excellence and efficiency. All while keeping a billion-dollar, eight-million-customer store up and available on a 24/7 basis.

Brand promise: Amazon.com is still a small and young company relative to the major offline retailers, and we must ensure that we build wide, strong customer relationships during this critical period.

Expanded product and service offerings: In 1999, we will continue to enhance the scope of our current product and service offerings, as well as add new initiatives. Amazon.com Auctions is our most recent addition. If any of you have not tried this new service, I encourage you to run—not walk—to www.amazon.com and click on the Auctions tab. As an Amazon.com customer, you are preregistered to both bid and sell. As a seller, you have access to Amazon.com's eight million experienced online shoppers.

Bench strength and processes: We've complicated our business dramatically with new products, services, geographies, acquisitions, and additions to our business model. We intend to invest in teams, processes, communication, and people-development practices. Scaling in this way is among the most challenging and difficult elements of our plan.

Amazon.com has made a number of strides forward in the past year, but there is still an enormous amount to learn and to do. We remain optimistic, but we also know we must remain vigilant and maintain a sense of urgency. We face many challenges and hurdles. Among them, aggressive, capable, and well-funded competition; the growth challenges and execution risk associated with our own expansion; and the need for large continuing investments to meet an expanding market opportunity.

The most important thing I could say in this letter was said in last year's letter, which detailed our long-term investment approach. Because we have so many new shareholders (this year we're printing more than two hundred thousand of these letters—last year we printed about thirteen thousand), we've appended last year's letter immediately after this year's. I invite you to please read the section titled "It's All About the Long Term." You might want to read it twice to make sure we're the kind of company you want to be invested in. As it says there, we don't claim it's the right philosophy, we just claim it's ours!

All the best and sincere thanks once again to our customers and shareholders and all the folks here who are working passionately every day to build an important and lasting company.

Building for the Long Term

1999

T HE FIRST FOUR and a half years of our journey have yielded some amazing results: we've now served over seventeen million customers in over 150 countries and built the leading global e-commerce brand and platform.

In the coming years we expect to benefit from the continued adoption of online commerce around the world as millions of new consumers connect to the Internet for the first time. As the online shopping experience continues to improve, consumer trust and confidence will increase, driving further adoption. And, if we at Amazon.com do our job right, we can be uniquely positioned to serve these new customers best and benefit as a result.

A Recap of 1999

During 1999, our relentless focus on customers worked:

Sales grew from $610 million in 1998 to $1.64 billion—a 169 percent increase.

We added 10.7 million new customers, increasing cumulative customer accounts from 6.2 million to 16.9 million.

The percentage of orders placed by repeat customers grew from over 64 percent in the fourth quarter of 1998 to greater than 73 percent in the same period in 1999.

Customers around the world are now choosing Amazon.com for a wide array of products. Only two years ago, Amazon.com's US book business represented 100 percent of our sales. Today, despite strong growth in US books, other areas account for more than half our sales. Major 1999 initiatives included Auctions, zShops, Toys, Consumer Electronics, Home Improvement, Software, Video Games, Payments, and our wireless initiative, Amazon Anywhere.

We've continued to be recognized as best-of-breed not only in our more established areas such as books, but in our newer stores as well. Just to focus on one area, Amazon Toys has received multiple awards, including being rated the best online toy store in an MSNBC survey, a ranking as the #1 online toy store by Forrester Research, and the top e-Rating from Consumer Reports in the toys category, in each case beating out a number of longer-established players.

Sales outside of the United States accounted for 22 percent of our business, totaling $358 million. In the United Kingdom and Germany, we added Music, Auctions, and zShops. In fact, Amazon. co.uk, Amazon.de, and Amazon.com are now the #1, #2, and #3 most popular online retail domains in Europe.

We grew worldwide distribution capacity from roughly three hundred thousand square feet to over five million square feet in less than twelve months.

In part because of this infrastructure, we were able to grow revenues 90 percent in just three months, while shipping well over 99 percent of our holiday orders in time for the holidays. As far as we can determine, no other company has ever grown 90 percent in three months on a sales base of over $1 billion.

I'm incredibly proud of everyone at Amazon.com for their tireless efforts to deliver what has become the standard-setting, Amazon.com-class customer experience while simultaneously handling such extraordinary growth rates. If any of you shareholders would like to thank this incredible worldwide team of Amazonians, please feel free to send an email to jeff@amazon.com. With help from my astounding office staff, I'll compile them and send them to the company. I know it would be appreciated. (As a side benefit I'll get to see if anyone reads these letters!)

In 1999, we continued to benefit from a business model that is inherently capital efficient. We don't need to build physical stores or stock those stores with inventory, and our centralized distribution model has allowed us to build a business with over $2 billion in annualized sales but requiring just $220 million in inventory and $318 million in fixed assets. Over the last five years, we've cumulatively used just $62 million in operating cash.

What Do You Own?

At a recent event at the Stanford University campus, a young woman came to the microphone and asked me a great question: "I have one hundred shares of Amazon.com. What do I own?"

I was surprised I hadn't heard it before, at least not so simply put. What do you own? You own a piece of the leading e-commerce platform.

The Amazon.com platform is comprised of brand, customers, technology, distribution capability, deep e-commerce expertise, and a great team with a passion for innovation and a passion for serving customers well. We begin the year 2000 with seventeen million customers, a worldwide reputation for customer focus, the best e-commerce software systems, and purpose-built distribution and customer service infrastructure. We believe we have reached a "tipping point," where this platform allows us to launch new ecommerce businesses faster, with a higher quality of customer experience, a lower incremental cost, a higher chance of success, and a faster path to scale and profitability than any other company.

Our vision is to use this platform to build Earth's most customer-centric company, a place where customers can come to find and discover anything and everything they might want to buy online. We won't do so alone but together with what will be thousands of partners of all sizes. We'll listen to customers, invent on their behalf, and personalize the store for each of them, all while working hard to continue to earn their trust. As is probably clear, this platform affords an unusually large-scale opportunity, one that should prove very valuable for both customers and shareholders if we can make the most of it. Despite the many risks and complexities, we are deeply committed to doing so.

Goals for 2000

In the year 2000, Amazon.com has six major goals: growth in both the number of our customers and the strength of the relationship we have with each of them; continued rapid expansion of the products and services we offer; driving operational excellence in all areas of the company; international expansion; expanding our partnership programs; and last, importantly, driving toward profitability in each and every business we are in. I'll spend a moment on each goal.

Growing and strengthening customer relationships: We will continue to invest heavily in introductions to new customers. Though it's sometimes hard to imagine with all that has happened in the last five years, this remains Day 1 for e-commerce, and these are the early days of category formation where many customers are forming relationships for the first time. We must work hard to grow the number of customers who shop with us, the number of products they purchase, the frequency with which they shop, and the level of satisfaction they have when they do so.

Product and service expansion: We are working to build a place where customers can find and discover anything they want to buy, anytime, anywhere. Each new product and service we offer makes us more relevant to a wider group of customers and can increase the frequency with which they visit our store. So, as we expand our offering, we create a virtuous cycle for the whole business. The more frequently customers visit our store, the less time, energy, and marketing investment is required to get them to come back again. In sight, in mind.

Further, as we expand, each new store has a dedicated team working to make it best-of-breed in its category; thus each new store is also a new opportunity to demonstrate to customers our focus on them. Finally, each new product or service further leverages our investments in distribution, customer service, technology, and brand, and can yield increased leverage on our bottom line.

Operational excellence: To us, operational excellence implies two things: delivering continuous improvement in customer experience and driving productivity, margin, efficiency, and asset velocity across all our businesses.

Often, the best way to drive one of these is to deliver the other. For instance, more efficient distribution yields faster delivery times, which in turn lowers contacts per order and customer service costs. These, in turn, improve customer experience and build brand, which in turn decreases customer acquisition and retention costs.

Our whole company is highly focused on driving operational excellence in each area of our business in 2000. Being world class in both customer experience and operations will allow us to grow faster and deliver even higher service levels.

International expansion: We think that consumers outside the United States are even more under-served by retail than those within it, and, with our platform in place, Amazon.com is well positioned to be a leading global retailer. We already have significant brand, sales, and customer presence around the world, as we've been shipping into over 150 countries for almost five years. I'm pleased to report that our stores in the United Kingdom and Germany are off to a strong start: they are already in the top ten web properties and the #1 e-commerce site in each of their respective countries. Our customers and shareholders around the world can look forward to further geographic expansion from this base during the coming year.

Expanding our partnership program: Through our platform, we are able to bring tremendous value to our partners, such as drugstore. com. In fact, our experience so far suggests that Amazon.com may easily be the most efficient, effective means for our partners to build their businesses. In many areas, partnering is the best way for us to rapidly expand our store in a customer-focused, cost-effective manner. One point worth emphasizing: the quality of customer experience a partner delivers is the single most important criteria in our selection process—we simply won't build a partnership with any company that does not share our passion for serving customers.

We love these kinds of partnerships because they please customers, please our partners, and are financially attractive, pleasing our shareholders: you and us.

Drive toward profitability in each business we are in: Each of the previous goals I've outlined contribute to our long-standing objective of building the best, most profitable, highest return on capital, long-term franchise. So in a way, driving profitability is the foundation underlying all of these goals. In the coming year, we expect to deliver substantial margin improvement and cost leverage as we drive continuous improvement in our partnerships with suppliers, in our own productivity and efficiency, in our management of fixed and working capital, and in our expertise in managing product mix and price.

Each successive product and service we launch this year should build on our platform, so our investment curve can be less steep and the time to profitability for each business should, in general, continue to shorten.

Taking the Long View

2000

OUCH. IT'S BEEN a brutal year for many in the capital markets and certainly for Amazon.com shareholders. As of this writing, our shares are down more than 80 percent from when I wrote you last year. Nevertheless, by almost any measure, Amazon.com the company is in a stronger position now than at any time in its past.

We served twenty million customers in 2000, up from fourteen million in 1999.

Sales grew to $2.76 billion in 2000 from $1.64 billion in 1999.

Pro forma operating loss shrank to 6 percent of sales in Q4 2000, from 26 percent of sales in Q4 1999.

Pro forma operating loss in the United States shrank to 2 percent of sales in Q4 2000, from 24 percent of sales in Q4 1999.

Average spend per customer in 2000 was $134, up 19 percent.

Gross profit grew to $656 million in 2000, from $291 million in 1999, up 125 percent.

Almost 36 percent of Q4 2000 US customers purchased from one of our "non-BMV" stores such as electronics, tools, and kitchen.

International sales grew to $381 million in 2000, from $168 million in 1999.

We helped our partner Toysrus.com sell more than $125 million
of toys and video games in Q4 2000.

We ended 2000 with cash and marketable securities of $1.1 bil-
lion, up from $706 million at the end of 1999, thanks to our early
2000 euroconvert financing.

And, most importantly, our heads-down focus on the customer
was reflected in a score of eighty-four on the American Customer
Satisfaction Index. We are told this is the highest score ever recorded
for a service company in any industry.

So, if the company is better positioned today than it was a year
ago, why is the stock price so much lower than it was a year ago? As
the famed investor Benjamin Graham said, "In the short term, the
stock market is a voting machine; in the long term, it's a weighing
machine." Clearly there was a lot of voting going on in the boom
year of '99—and much less weighing. We're a company that wants to
be weighed, and over time, we will be—over the long term, all companies are. In the meantime, we have our heads down working to
build a heavier and heavier company.

Many of you have heard me talk about the "bold bets" that we as
a company have made and will continue to make—these bold bets
have included everything from our investment in digital and wireless technologies, to our decision to invest in smaller e-commerce
companies, including living.com and Pets.com, both of which shut
down operations in 2000. We were significant shareholders in both
and lost a significant amount of money on both.

We made these investments because we knew we wouldn't ourselves be entering these particular categories any time soon, and we
believed passionately in the "land rush" metaphor for the Internet.
Indeed, that metaphor was an extraordinarily useful decision aid
for several years starting in 1994, but we now believe its usefulness
largely faded away over the last couple of years. In retrospect, we
significantly underestimated how much time would be available to

enter these categories and underestimated how difficult it would be for single-category e-commerce companies to achieve the scale necessary to succeed.

Online selling (relative to traditional retailing) is a scale business characterized by high fixed costs and relatively low variable costs. This makes it difficult to be a medium-sized e-commerce company. With a long enough financing runway, Pets.com and living.com may have been able to acquire enough customers to achieve the needed scale. But when the capital markets closed the door on financing Internet companies, these companies simply had no choice but to close their doors. As painful as that was, the alternative—investing more of our own capital in these companies to keep them afloat—would have been an even bigger mistake.

Future: Real Estate Doesn't Obey Moore's Law

Let's move to the future. Why should you be optimistic about the future of e-commerce and the future of Amazon.com?

Industry growth and new customer adoption will be driven over the coming years by relentless improvements in the customer experience of online shopping. These improvements in customer experience will be driven by innovations made possible by dramatic increases in available bandwidth, disk space, and processing power, all of which are getting cheap fast.

Price performance of processing power is doubling about every eighteen months (Moore's Law), price performance of disk space is doubling about every twelve months, and price performance of bandwidth is doubling about every nine months. Given that last doubling rate, Amazon.com will be able to use sixty times as much bandwidth per customer five years from now while holding our bandwidth cost per customer constant. Similarly, price performance improvements in disk space and processing power will allow us to, for example, do ever more and better real-time personalization of our website.

In the physical world, retailers will continue to use technology to reduce costs, but not to transform the customer experience. We too will use technology to reduce costs, but the bigger effect will be using technology to drive adoption and revenue. We still believe that some 15 percent of retail commerce may ultimately move online.

While there are no foregone conclusions, and we still have much to prove, Amazon.com today is a unique asset. We have the brand, the customer relationships, the technology, the fulfillment infrastructure, the financial strength, the people, and the determination to extend our leadership in this infant industry and to build an important and lasting company. And we will do so by keeping the customer first.

The year 2001 will be an important one in our development. Like 2000, this year will be a year of focus and execution. As a first step, we've set the goal of achieving a pro forma operating profit in the fourth quarter. While we have a tremendous amount of work to do and there can be no guarantees, we have a plan to get there, it's our top priority, and every person in this company is committed to helping with that goal. I look forward to reporting to you our progress in the coming year.

We at Amazon.com remain grateful to our customers for their business and trust, to each other for our hard work, and to our shareholders for their support and encouragement. Many, many thanks.

The Customer Franchise Is Our Most Valuable Asset

2001

In July of last year, Amazon.com reached an important way station. After four years of single-minded focus on growth, and then just under two years spent almost exclusively on lowering costs, we reached a point where we could afford to balance growth and cost improvement, dedicating resources and staffed projects to both. Our major price reduction in July, moving to discount books over $20 by 30 percent off list, marked this change.

This balance began to pay off in the fourth quarter, when we both significantly exceeded our own goals on the bottom line and simultaneously reaccelerated growth in our business. We lowered prices again in January when we offered a new class of shipping that is free (year-round) on orders over $99. Focus on cost improvement makes it possible for us to afford to lower prices, which drives growth. Growth spreads fixed costs across more sales, reducing cost per unit, which makes possible more price reductions. Customers like this, and it's good for shareholders. Please expect us to repeat this loop.

As I mentioned, we exceeded our goals for the fourth quarter with pro forma operating profit of $59 million and pro forma net profit of $35 million. Thousands of Amazon.com employees around the world worked hard to achieve that goal; they are, and should be, proud of the accomplishment. More highlights from a notable year:

Sales grew 13 percent from $2.76 billion in 2000 to $3.12 billion in 2001; we achieved our first billion-dollar quarter on reaccelerated sales and 23 percent year-over-year unit growth in Q4.

We served twenty-five million customer accounts in 2001, compared to twenty million in 2000 and fourteen million in 1999.

International sales grew 74 percent in 2001, and more than one-quarter of sales came from outside the United States. The United Kingdom and Germany, our largest international markets, had a combined pro forma operating profit for the first time in Q4. Open only a year, Japan grew to a $100 million annual run rate in Q4.

Hundreds of thousands of small businesses and individuals made money by selling new and used products to our customers directly from our highly trafficked product detail pages. These Marketplace orders grew to 15 percent of US orders in Q4, far surpassing our expectations when we launched Marketplace in November 2000.

Inventory turns increased from twelve in 2000 to sixteen in 2001.

Most important, we stayed relentlessly focused on the customer, as reflected in a chart-topping score of eighty-four for the second year in a row on the widely followed American Customer Satisfaction Index conducted by the University of Michigan. We are told this is the highest score ever recorded—not just for any retailer, but for any service company.

Obsess over Customers: Our Commitment Continues

Until July, Amazon.com had been primarily built on two pillars of customer experience: selection and convenience. In July, as I already discussed, we added a third customer experience pillar: relentlessly lowering prices. You should know that our commitment to the first two pillars remains as strong as ever.

We now have more than forty-five thousand items in our electronics store (about seven times the selection you're likely to find in a big-box electronics store), we've tripled our kitchen selection (you'll find all the best brands), we've launched computer and magazine subscriptions stores, and we've added selection with strategic partners such as Target and Circuit City.

We've improved convenience with features like Instant Order Update, which warns you if you're about to buy the same item twice (people are busy—they forget that they've already bought it!).

We've dramatically improved customer self-service capabilities. Customers can now easily find, cancel, or modify their own orders. To find an order, just make sure you are signed in and recognized by the site, and do a regular search on any product in your order. When you get to that product's detail page, a link to your order will be at the top of the page.

We built a new feature called Look Inside the Book. Customers can view large high-resolution images of not only the front cover of a book but also the back cover, index, table of contents, and a reasonable sample of the inside pages. They can Look Inside the Book before making a buying decision. It's available on over two hundred thousand of our millions of titles (as a point of comparison, a typical book superstore carries about one hundred thousand titles).

As my last example, I'll just point out that one of the most important things we've done to improve convenience and experience for customers also happens to be a huge driver of variable cost productivity: eliminating mistakes and errors at their root. Every year that's gone by since Amazon.com's founding, we've done a better and better job of eliminating errors, and this past year was our best ever. Eliminating the root causes of errors saves us money and saves customers time.

Our consumer franchise is our most valuable asset, and we will nourish it with innovation and hard work.

An Investment Framework

In every annual letter (including this one), we attach a copy of our original 1997 letter to shareholders to help investors decide if Amazon.com is the right kind of investment for them, and to help us determine if we have remained true to our original goals and values. I think we have.

In that 1997 letter, we wrote, "When forced to choose between optimizing the appearance of our GAAP accounting and maximizing the present value of future cash flows, we'll take the cash flows."

Why focus on cash flows? Because a share of stock is a share of a company's future cash flows, and, as a result, cash flows more than any other single variable seem to do the best job of explaining a company's stock price over the long term.

If you could know for certain just two things—a company's future cash flows and its future number of shares outstanding—you would have an excellent idea of the fair value of a share of that company's stock today. (You'd also need to know appropriate discount rates, but if you knew the future cash flows *for certain*, it would also be reasonably easy to know which discount rates to use.) It's not easy, but you can make an informed forecast of future cash flows by examining a company's performance in the past and by looking at factors such as the leverage points and scalability in that company's model. Estimating the number of shares outstanding in the future requires you to forecast items such as option grants to employees or other potential capital transactions. Ultimately, your determination of cash flow per share will be a strong indicator of the price you might be willing to pay for a share of ownership in any company.

Since we expect to keep our fixed costs largely fixed, even at significantly higher unit volumes, we believe Amazon.com is poised over the coming years to generate meaningful, sustained, free cash flow. Our goal for 2002 reflects just that. As we said in January when we reported our fourth quarter results, we plan this year to generate positive operating cash flow, leading to free cash flow (the difference between the two is up to $75 million of planned capital expenditures). Our trailing twelve-month pro forma net income should, roughly but not perfectly, trend like trailing twelve-month cash flow.

Limiting share count means more cash flow per share and more long-term value for owners. Our current objective is to target net dilution from employee stock options (grants net of cancellations) to an average of 3 percent per year over the next five years, although in any given year it might be higher or lower.

Relentless Commitment to Long-Term Shareholder Value

As I've discussed many times before, we are firm believers that the long-term interests of shareholders are tightly linked to the interests of our customers: if we do our jobs right, today's customers will buy more tomorrow, we'll add more customers in the process, and it will all add up to more cash flow and more long-term value for our shareholders. To that end, we are committed to extending our leadership in e-commerce in a way that benefits customers and therefore, inherently, investors—you can't do one without the other.

As we kick off 2002, I am happy to report that I am as enthusiastic as ever about this business. There is more innovation ahead of us than behind us, we are close to demonstrating the operating leverage of our business model, and I get to work with this amazing team of Amazonians all over the world. I am lucky and grateful. We thank you, our owners, for your support, your encouragement, and for joining us on this adventure. If you're a customer, we thank you again!

What's Good for Customers Is Good for Shareholders

2002

I N MANY WAYS, Amazon.com is not a normal store. We have deep selection that is unconstrained by shelf space. We turn our inventory nineteen times in a year. We personalize the store for each and every customer. We trade real estate for technology (which gets cheaper and more capable every year). We display customer reviews critical of our products. You can make a purchase with a few seconds and one click. We put used products next to new ones so you can choose. We share our prime real estate—our product detail pages—with third parties, and, if they can offer better value, we let them.

One of our most exciting peculiarities is poorly understood. People see that we're determined to offer both world-leading customer experience *and* the lowest possible prices, but to some this dual goal seems paradoxical if not downright quixotic. Traditional stores face a time-tested trade-off between offering high-touch customer experience on the one hand and the lowest possible prices on the other. How can Amazon.com be trying to do both?

The answer is that we transform much of customer experience—such as unmatched selection, extensive product information, personalized recommendations, and other new software features—into largely a fixed expense. With customer experience costs largely fixed (more like a publishing model than a retailing model), our costs as a percentage of sales can shrink rapidly as we grow our business. Moreover, customer experience costs that remain variable—such as the variable portion of fulfillment costs—improve in our model as we reduce defects. Eliminating defects improves costs and leads to better customer experience.

We believe our ability to lower prices and simultaneously drive customer experience is a big deal, and this past year offers evidence that the strategy is working.

First, we do continue to drive customer experience. The holiday season this year is one example. While delivering a record number of units to customers, we also delivered our best-ever experience. Cycle time, the amount of time taken by our fulfillment centers to process an order, improved 17 percent compared with last year. And our most sensitive measure of customer satisfaction, contacts per order, saw a 13 percent improvement.

Inside existing product categories, we've worked hard to increase selection. Electronics selection is up over 40 percent in the United States alone over the prior year, and we now offer ten times the selection of a typical big box electronics store. Even in US books, where we've been working for eight years, we increased selection by 15 percent, mostly in harder-to-find and out-of-print titles. And, of course, we've added new categories. Our Apparel and Accessories store has more than five hundred top clothing brands, and in its first sixty days, customers bought 153,000 shirts, 106,000 pairs of pants, and 31,000 pairs of underwear.

In this year's American Customer Satisfaction Index, the most authoritative study of customer satisfaction, Amazon.com scored an eighty-eight, the highest score ever recorded—not just online, not just in retailing—but the highest score ever recorded in any service industry. In ACSI's words, "Amazon.com continues to show remarkably high levels of customer satisfaction. With a score of 88 (up 5%), it is generating satisfaction at a level unheard of in the service industry. . . . Can customer satisfaction for Amazon climb more? The latest ACSI data suggest that it is indeed possible. Both service and the value proposition offered by Amazon have increased at a steep rate."

Second, while focused on customer experience, we've also been lowering prices substantially. We've been doing so broadly across product categories, from books to electronics, and we've eliminated shipping fees with our 365-day-per-year Free Super Saver Shipping on orders over $25. We've been taking similar actions in every country in which we do business.

Our pricing objective is not to discount a small number of products for a limited period of time, but to offer low prices every day and apply them broadly across our entire product range. To illustrate this point, we recently did a price comparison versus a major well-known chain of book superstores. We did not hand pick a choice group of books against which we wanted to compare. Instead, we used their published list of their one hundred bestsellers for 2002. It was a good representation of the kinds of books people buy most, consisting of forty-five hardcover titles and fifty-five paperbacks across many different categories, including Literature, Romance, Mystery and Thrillers, Nonfiction, Children's, Self-Help, and so on.

We priced all one hundred titles by visiting their superstores in both Seattle and New York City. It took us six hours in four of their different superstores to find all one hundred books on their list. When we added up everything we spent, we discovered that:

At their stores, these one hundred bestselling books cost $1,561. At Amazon.com, the same books cost $1,195 for a total savings of $366, or 23 percent.

For seventy-two of the one hundred books, our price was cheaper. On twenty-five of the books, our price was the same. On three of the one hundred, their prices were better (we subsequently reduced our prices on these three books).

In these physical-world superstores, only fifteen of their one hundred titles were discounted—they were selling the other eighty-five at full list price. At Amazon.com, seventy-six of the one hundred were discounted, and twenty-four were sold at list price.

To be sure, you may find reasons to shop in the physical world—for instance, if you need something immediately—but, if you do so, you'll be paying a premium. If you want to save money and time, you'll do better by shopping at Amazon.com.

Third, our determination to deliver low price *and* customer experience is generating financial results. Net sales this year increased 26 percent to a record $3.9 billion, and unit sales grew at an even faster 34 percent. Free cash flow—our most important financial measure—reached $135 million, a $305 million improvement over the prior year.*

In short, what's good for customers is good for shareholders.

Once again this year, I attach a copy of our original 1997 letter and encourage current and prospective shareowners to take a look at it. Given how much we've grown and how much the Internet has evolved, it's notable that the fundamentals of how we do business remain the same.

---

*Free cash flow for 2002 of $135 million is net cash provided by operating activities of $174 million less purchases of fixed assets of $39 million. Free cash flow for 2001 of negative $170 million is net cash used in operating activities of $120 million less purchases of fixed assets of $50 million.

Long-Term Thinking

2003

LONG-TERM THINKING IS both a requirement and an outcome of true ownership. Owners are different from tenants. I know of a couple who rented out their house, and the family who moved in nailed their Christmas tree to the hardwood floors instead of using a tree stand. Expedient, I suppose, and admittedly these were particularly bad tenants, but no owner would be so short-sighted. Similarly, many investors are effectively short-term tenants, turning their portfolios so quickly they are really just renting the stocks that they temporarily "own."

We emphasized our long-term views in our 1997 letter to shareholders, our first as a public company, because that approach really does drive making many concrete, nonabstract decisions. I'd like to discuss a few of these nonabstract decisions in the context of customer experience. At Amazon.com, we use the term customer experience broadly. It includes every customer-facing aspect of our business—from our product prices to our selection, from our website's user interface to how we package and ship items. The customer experience we create is by far the most important driver of our business.

As we design our customer experience, we do so with long-term owners in mind. We try to make all of our customer experience decisions—big and small—in that framework.

For instance, shortly after launching Amazon.com in 1995, we empowered customers to review products. While now a routine Amazon.com practice, at the time we received complaints from a few vendors, basically wondering if we understood our business: "You make money when you sell things—why would you allow negative reviews on your website?" Speaking as a focus group of one, I know I've sometimes changed my mind before making purchases on Amazon.com as a result of negative or lukewarm customer reviews. Though negative reviews cost us some sales in the short term, helping customers make better purchase decisions ultimately pays off for the company.

Another example is our Instant Order Update feature, which reminds you that you've already bought a particular item. Customers lead busy lives and cannot always remember if they've already purchased a particular item, say a DVD or CD they bought a year earlier. When we launched Instant Order Update, we were able to measure with statistical significance that the feature slightly reduced sales. Good for customers? Definitely. Good for shareowners? Yes, in the long run.

Among the most expensive customer experience improvements we're focused on are our everyday free shipping offers and our ongoing product price reductions. Eliminating defects, improving productivity, and passing the resulting cost savings back to customers in the form of lower prices is a long-term decision. Increased volumes take time to materialize, and price reductions almost always hurt current results. In the long term, however, relentlessly driving the "price-cost structure loop" will leave us with a stronger, more valuable business. Since many of our costs, such as software engineering, are relatively fixed and many of our variable costs can also be better managed at larger scale, driving more volume through our cost structure reduces those costs as a percentage of sales. To give one small example, engineering a feature like Instant Order Update for use by forty million customers costs nowhere near forty times what it would cost to do the same for one million customers.

Our pricing strategy does not attempt to maximize margin *percentages*, but instead seeks to drive maximum value for customers and thereby create a much larger bottom line—in the long term. For example, we're targeting gross margins on our jewelry sales to be substantially lower than industry norms because we believe over time—customers figure these things out—this approach will produce more value for shareholders.

We have a strong team of hard-working, innovative folks building Amazon.com. They are focused on the customer and focused on the long term. On that time scale, the interests of shareowners and customers are aligned.

P.S. Again this year, the widely followed American Customer Satisfaction Index gave Amazon.com a score of eighty-eight—the highest customer satisfaction score ever recorded in any service industry, online or off. A representative of the ACSI was quoted as saying, "If they go any higher, they will get a nosebleed." We're working on that.

Thinking About Finance

2004

O UR ULTIMATE FINANCIAL measure, and the one we most want to drive over the long-term, is free cash flow per share.

Why not focus first and foremost, as many do, on earnings, earnings per share or earnings growth? The simple answer is that earnings don't directly translate into cash flows, and shares are worth only the present value of their future cash flows, not the present value of their future earnings. Future earnings are a component—but not the only important component—of future cash flow per share. Working capital and capital expenditures are also important, as is future share dilution.

Though some may find it counterintuitive, a company can actually impair shareholder value in certain circumstances by growing earnings. This happens when the capital investments required for growth exceed the present value of the cash flow derived from those investments.

To illustrate with a hypothetical and very simplified example, imagine that an entrepreneur invents a machine that can quickly transport people from one location to another. The machine is expensive—$160 million with an annual capacity of one hundred thousand passenger trips and a four-year useful life. Each trip sells for $1,000 and requires $450 in cost of goods for energy and materials and $50 in labor and other costs.

Continue to imagine that business is booming, with one hundred thousand trips in Year 1, completely and perfectly utilizing the capacity of one machine. This leads to earnings of $10 million after deducting operating expenses including depreciation—a 10 percent net margin. The company's primary focus is on earnings; so based on initial results the entrepreneur decides to invest more capital to fuel sales and earnings growth, adding additional machines in Years 2 through 4.

Here are the income statements for the first four years of business:

	Earnings (in thousands)			
	Year 1	**Year 2**	**Year 3**	**Year 4**
Sales	$100,000	$200,000	$400,000	$800,000
Units Sold	100	200	400	800
Growth	N/A	100%	100%	100%
Gross profit	55,000	110,000	220,000	440,000
Gross margin	55%	55%	55%	55%
Depreciation	40,000	80,000	160,000	320,000
Labor and other costs	5,000	10,000	20,000	40,000
Earning	$ 10,000	$ 20,000	$ 40,000	$ 80,000
Margin	10%	10%	10%	10%
Growth	N/A	100%	100%	100%

It's impressive: 100 percent compound earnings growth and $150 million of cumulative earnings. Investors considering only the above income statement would be delighted.

However, looking at cash flows tells a different story. Over the same four years, the transportation business generates cumulative negative free cash flow of $530 million.

	Cash Flow (in thousands)			
	Year 1	Year 2	Year 3	Year 4
Earnings	$10,000	$20,000	$40,000	$80,000
Depreciation	40,000	80,000	160,000	320,000
Working Capital	–	–	–	–
Operational Cash Flow	50,000	100,000	200,000	400,000
Capital Expenditures	160,000	160,000	320,000	640,000
Free Cash Flow	$(110,000)	$ (60,000)	$(120,000)	$(240,000)

There are of course other business models where earnings more closely approximate cash flows. But as our transportation example illustrates, one cannot assess the creation or destruction of shareholder value with certainty by looking at the income statement alone.

Notice, too, that a focus on EBITDA (earnings before interest, taxes, depreciation, and amortization) would lead to the same faulty conclusion about the health of the business. Sequential annual EBITDA would have been $50, $100, $200 and $400 million—100 percent growth for three straight years. But without taking into account the $1.28 billion in capital expenditures necessary to generate this "cash flow," we're getting only part of the story—EBITDA isn't cash flow.

What if we modified the growth rates and, correspondingly, capital expenditures for machinery—would cash flows have deteriorated or improved?

Year 2, 3, and 4 Sales and Earnings Growth Rate	Number of Machines in Year 4	Year 1 to 4 Cumulative Earnings	Year 1 to 4 Cumulative Free Cash Flow
		(in thousands)	
0%, 0%, 0%	1	$ 40,000	$ 40,000
100%, 50%, 33%	4	$100,000	$(140,000)
100%, 100%, 100%	8	$150,000	$(530,000)

Paradoxically, from a cash flow perspective, the slower this business grows the better off it is. Once the initial capital outlay has been made for the first machine, the ideal growth trajectory is to scale to 100 percent of capacity quickly, then stop growing. However, even with only one piece of machinery, the gross cumulative cash flow doesn't surpass the initial machine cost until Year 4 and the net present value of this stream of cash flows (using 12 percent cost of capital) is still negative.

Unfortunately our transportation business is fundamentally flawed. There is no growth rate at which it makes sense to invest initial or subsequent capital to operate the business. In fact, our example is so simple and clear as to be obvious. Investors would run a net present value analysis on the economics and quickly determine it doesn't pencil out. Though it's more subtle and complex in the real world, this issue—the duality between earnings and cash flows—comes up all the time.

Cash flow statements often don't receive as much attention as they deserve. Discerning investors don't stop with the income statement.

Our Most Important Financial Measure: Free Cash Flow per Share

Amazon.com's financial focus is on long-term growth in free cash flow per share. Amazon.com's free cash flow is driven primarily by increasing operating profit dollars and efficiently managing both working capital and capital expenditures. We work to increase operating profit by focusing on improving all aspects of the customer experience to grow sales and by maintaining a lean cost structure.

We have a cash generative operating cycle* because we turn our inventory quickly, collecting payments from our customers before

---

*The operating cycle is number of days of sales in inventory plus number of days of sales in accounts receivable minus accounts payable days.

payments are due to suppliers. Our high inventory turnover means we maintain relatively low levels of investment in inventory—$480 million at year end on a sales base of nearly $7 billion.

The capital efficiency of our business model is illustrated by our modest investments in fixed assets, which were $246 million at year end or 4 percent of 2004 sales.

Free cash flow* grew 38 percent to $477 million in 2004, a $131 million improvement over the prior year. We are confident that if we continue to improve customer experience—including increasing selection and lowering prices—and execute efficiently, our value proposition, as well as our free cash flow, will further expand.

As to dilution, total shares outstanding plus stock-based awards are essentially unchanged at the end of 2004, compared with 2003, and are down 1 percent over the last three years. During that same period, we've also eliminated over six million shares of potential future dilution by repaying more than $600 million of convertible debt that was due in 2009 and 2010. Efficiently managing share count means more cash flow per share and more long-term value for owners.

This focus on free cash flow isn't new for Amazon.com. We made it clear in our 1997 letter to shareholders—our first as a public company—that when "forced to choose between optimizing GAAP accounting and maximizing the present value of future cash flows, we'll take the cash flows."

---

*Free cash flow is defined as net cash provided by operating activities less purchases of fixed assets, including capitalized internal-use software and website development, both of which are presented on our statements of cash flows. Free cash flow for 2004 of $477 million is net cash provided by operating activities of $567 million less purchases of fixed assets, including capitalized internal-use software and website development costs, of $89 million. Free cash flow for 2003 of $346 million is net cash provided by operating activities of $392 million less purchases of fixed assets, including capitalized internal-use software and website development costs, of $46 million.

Making Decisions

2005

M ANY OF THE important decisions we make at Amazon.com can be made with data. There is a right answer or a wrong answer, a better answer or a worse answer, and math tells us which is which. These are our favorite kinds of decisions.

Opening a new fulfillment center is an example. We use history from our existing fulfillment network to estimate seasonal peaks and to model alternatives for new capacity. We look at anticipated product mix, including product dimensions and weight, to decide how much space we need and whether we need a facility for smaller "sortable" items or for larger items that usually ship alone. To shorten delivery times and reduce outbound transportation costs, we analyze prospective locations based on proximity to customers, transportation hubs, and existing facilities. Quantitative analysis improves the customer's experience and our cost structure.

Similarly, most of our inventory purchase decisions can be numerically modeled and analyzed. We want products in stock and immediately available to customers, and we want minimal total inventory in order to keep associated holding costs, and thus prices, low. To achieve both, there is a right amount of inventory. We use historical purchase data to forecast customer demand for a product and expected variability in that demand. We use data on the historical performance of vendors to estimate replenishment times. We can determine where to stock the product within our fulfillment network based on inbound and outbound transportation costs, storage costs, and anticipated customer locations. With this approach, we keep over one million unique items under our own roof, immediately available for customers, while still turning inventory more than fourteen times per year.

The above decisions require us to make some assumptions and judgments, but in such decisions, judgment and opinion come into play only as junior partners. The heavy lifting is done by the math.

As you would expect, however, not all of our important decisions can be made in this enviable, math-based way. Sometimes we have little or no historical data to guide us and proactive experimentation is impossible, impractical, or tantamount to a decision to proceed. Though data, analysis, and math play a role, the prime ingredient in these decisions is judgment.*

As our shareholders know, we have made a decision to continuously and significantly lower prices for customers year after year as our efficiency and scale make it possible. This is an example of a very important decision that cannot be made in a math-based way. In fact, when we lower prices, we go against the math that we can

---

*"The Structure of 'Unstructured' Decision Processes" is a fascinating 1976 paper by Henry Mintzberg, Duru Raisinghani, and Andre Theoret. They look at how institutions make strategic, "unstructured" decisions as opposed to more quantifiable "operating" decisions. Among other gems you will find in the paper is this: "Excessive attention by management scientists to operating decisions may well cause organizations to pursue inappropriate courses of action more efficiently." They are not debating the importance of rigorous and quantitative analysis, but only noting that it gets a lopsided amount of study and attention, probably because of the very fact that it is more quantifiable. The whole paper is available at www.amazon.com/ir/mintzberg.

do, which always says that the smart move is to *raise* prices. We have significant data related to price elasticity. With fair accuracy, we can predict that a price reduction of a certain percentage will result in an increase in units sold of a certain percentage. With rare exceptions, the volume increase in the short term is never enough to pay for the price decrease. However, our quantitative understanding of elasticity is short-term. We can estimate what a price reduction will do this week and this quarter. But we cannot numerically estimate the effect that consistently lowering prices will have on our business over five years or ten years or more. Our *judgment* is that relentlessly returning efficiency improvements and scale economies to customers in the form of lower prices creates a virtuous cycle that leads over the long term to a much larger dollar amount of free cash flow, and thereby to a much more valuable Amazon.com. We've made similar judgments around Free Super Saver Shipping and Amazon Prime, both of which are expensive in the short term and—we believe—important and valuable in the long term.

As another example, in 2000 we invited third parties to compete directly against us on our "prime retail real estate"—our product detail pages. Launching a single detail page for both Amazon retail and third-party items seemed risky. Well-meaning people internally and externally worried it would cannibalize Amazon's retail business, and—as is often the case with consumer-focused innovations—there was no way to prove in advance that it would work. Our buyers pointed out that inviting third parties onto Amazon.com would make inventory forecasting more difficult and that we could get "stuck" with excess inventory if we "lost the detail page" to one of our third-party sellers. However, our judgment was simple. If a third party could offer a better price or better availability on a particular item, then we wanted our customer to get easy access to that offer. Over time, third-party sales have become a successful and significant part of our business. Third-party units have grown from 6 percent of total units sold in 2000 to 28 percent in 2005, even as retail revenues have grown threefold.

Math-based decisions command wide agreement, whereas judgment-based decisions are rightly debated and often controversial, at least until put into practice and demonstrated. Any institution unwilling to endure controversy must limit itself to decisions of the first type. In our view, doing so would not only limit controversy—it would also significantly limit innovation and long-term value creation.

The foundation of our decision-making philosophy was laid out in our 1997 letter to shareholders, a copy of which is attached:

We will continue to focus relentlessly on our customers.

We will continue to make investment decisions in light of long-term market leadership considerations rather than short-term profitability considerations or short-term Wall Street reactions.

We will continue to measure our programs and the effectiveness of our investments analytically, to jettison those that do not provide acceptable returns, and to step up our investment in those that work best. We will continue to learn from both our successes and our failures.

We will make bold rather than timid investment decisions where we see a sufficient probability of gaining market leadership advantages. Some of these investments will pay off, others will not, and we will have learned another valuable lesson in either case.

You can count on us to combine a strong quantitative and analytical culture with a willingness to make bold decisions. As we do so, we'll start with the customer and work backward. In our judgment, that is the best way to create shareholder value.

Growing New Businesses

2006

A T AMAZON'S CURRENT scale, planting seeds that will grow into meaningful new businesses takes some discipline, a bit of patience, and a nurturing culture.

Our established businesses are well-rooted young trees. They are growing, enjoy high returns on capital, and operate in very large market segments. These characteristics set a high bar for any new business we would start. Before we invest our shareholders' money in a new business, we must convince ourselves that the new opportunity can generate the returns on capital our investors expected when they invested in Amazon. And we must convince ourselves that the new business can grow to a scale where it can be significant in the context of our overall company.

Furthermore, we must believe that the opportunity is currently underserved and that we have the capabilities needed to bring strong customer-facing differentiation to the marketplace. Without that, it's unlikely we'd get to scale in that new business.

I often get asked, "When are you going to open physical stores?" That's an expansion opportunity we've resisted. It fails all but one of the tests outlined above. The potential size of a network of physical stores is exciting. However, we don't know how to do it with low capital and high returns; physical-world retailing is a cagey and ancient business that's already well served; and we don't have any ideas for how to build a physical world store experience that's meaningfully differentiated for customers.

When you do see us enter new businesses, it's because we believe the above tests have been passed. Our acquisition of Joyo.com is a first step in serving the most populous country in the world. E-commerce in China is still in its early days, and we believe it's an excellent business opportunity. Shoes, apparel, groceries: these are big segments where we have the right skills to invent and grow large-scale, high-return businesses that genuinely improve customer experience.

Fulfillment by Amazon is a set of web services APIs that turns our twelve million square foot fulfillment center network into a gigantic and sophisticated computer peripheral. Pay us forty-five cents per month per cubic foot of fulfillment center space, and you can stow your products in our network. You make web services calls to alert us to expect inventory to arrive, to tell us to pick and pack one or more items, and to tell us where to ship those items. You never have to talk to us. It's differentiated, can be large, and passes our returns bar.

Amazon Web Services is another example. With AWS, we're building a new business focused on a new customer set: software developers. We currently offer ten different web services and have built a community of over 240,000 registered developers. We're targeting broad needs universally faced by developers, such as storage and compute capacity—areas in which developers have asked for help, and in which we have deep expertise from scaling Amazon .com over the last twelve years. We're well positioned to do it, it's highly differentiated, and it can be a significant, financially attractive business over time.

In some large companies, it might be difficult to grow new businesses from tiny seeds because of the patience and nurturing required. In my view, Amazon's culture is unusually supportive of small businesses with big potential, and I believe that's a source of competitive advantage.

Like any company, we have a corporate culture formed not only by our intentions but also as a result of our history. For Amazon, that history is fairly fresh and, fortunately, it includes several examples of tiny seeds growing into big trees. We have many people at our company who have watched multiple $10 million seeds turn into billion-dollar businesses. That firsthand experience and the culture that has grown up around those successes is, in my opinion, a big part of why we can start businesses from scratch. The culture demands that these new businesses be high potential and that they be innovative and differentiated, but it does not demand that they be large on the day that they are born.

I remember how excited we were in 1996 as we crossed $10 million in book sales. It wasn't hard to be excited—we had grown to $10 million from zero. Today, when a new business inside Amazon grows to $10 million, the overall company is growing from $10 billion to $10.01 billion. It would be easy for the senior executives who run our established billion-dollar businesses to scoff. But they don't. They watch the growth rates of the emerging businesses and send emails of congratulations. That's pretty cool, and we're proud it's a part of our culture.

In our experience, if a new business enjoys runaway success, it can only *begin* to be meaningful to the overall company economics in something like three to seven years. We've seen those time frames with our international businesses, our earlier nonmedia businesses, and our third-party seller businesses. Today, international is 45 percent of sales, nonmedia is 34 percent of sales, and our third-party seller businesses account for 28 percent of our units sold. We will be happy indeed if some of the new seeds we're planting enjoy similar successes.

We've come a distance since we celebrated our first $10 million in sales. As we continue to grow, we'll work to maintain a culture that embraces new businesses. We will do so in a disciplined way, with an eye on returns, potential size, and the ability to create differentiation that customers care about. We won't always choose right, and we won't always succeed. But we will be choosy, and we will work hard and patiently.

A Team of Missionaries

2007

NOVEMBER 19, 2007, was a special day. After three years of work, we introduced Amazon Kindle to our customers.

Many of you may already know something of Kindle—we're fortunate (and grateful) that it has been broadly written and talked about. Briefly, Kindle is a purpose-built reading device with wireless access to more than 110,000 books, blogs, magazines, and newspapers. The wireless connectivity isn't Wi-Fi—instead it uses the same wireless network as advanced cell phones, which means it works when you're at home in bed or out and moving around. You can buy a book directly from the device, and the whole book will be downloaded wirelessly, ready for reading, in less than sixty seconds. There is no "wireless plan," no yearlong contract you must commit to, and no monthly service fee. It has a paper-like electronic-ink display that's easy to read even in bright daylight. Folks who see the display for the first time do a double take. It's thinner and lighter than a paperback and can hold two hundred books. Take a look at the Kindle detail page on Amazon.com to see what customers think—Kindle has already been reviewed more than two thousand times.

As you might expect after three years of work, we had sincere hopes that Kindle would be well received, but we did not expect the level of demand that actually materialized. We sold out in the first five and a half hours, and our supply chain and manufacturing teams have had to scramble to increase production capacity.

We started by setting ourselves the admittedly audacious goal of improving upon the physical book. We did not choose that goal lightly. Anything that has persisted in roughly the same form and re-sisted change for five hundred years is unlikely to be improved easily. At the beginning of our design process, we identified what we believe is the book's most important feature. It *disappears*. When you read a book, you don't notice the paper and the ink and the glue and the stitching. All of that dissolves, and what remains is the author's world.

We knew Kindle would have to *get out of the way*, just like a phys-ical book, so readers could become engrossed in the words and for-get they're reading on a device. We also knew we shouldn't try to copy every last feature of a book—we could never out-book the book. We'd have to add *new* capabilities—ones that could never be possible with a traditional book.

The early days of Amazon.com provide an analog. It was tempt-ing back then to believe that an online bookstore should have all the features of a physical bookstore. I was asked about a particu-lar feature dozens of times: "How are you going to do electronic book signings?" Thirteen years later, we still haven't figured that one out! Instead of trying to duplicate physical bookstores, we've been inspired by them and worked to find things we could do in the new medium that could never be done in the old one. We don't have electronic book signings, and similarly we can't provide a com-fortable spot to sip coffee and relax. However, we can offer literally *millions* of titles, help with purchase decisions through customer re-views, and provide discovery features like "customers who bought this item also bought." The list of useful things that can be done only in the new medium is a long one.

I'll highlight a few of the useful features we built into Kindle that go beyond what you could ever do with a physical book. If you come across a word you don't recognize, you can look it up easily. You can search your books. Your margin notes and underlinings are stored on the server-side in the "cloud," where they can't be lost. Kindle keeps your place in each of the books you're reading, automatically. If your eyes are tired, you can change the font size. Most important is the seamless, simple ability to find a book and have it in sixty seconds. When I've watched people do this for the first time, it's clear the capability has a profound effect on them. Our vision for Kindle is every book ever printed in any language, all available in less than sixty seconds. Publishers—including all the major publishers—have embraced Kindle, and we're thankful for that. From a publisher's point of view, there are a lot of advantages to Kindle. Books never go out of print, and they never go out of stock. Nor is there ever waste from overprinting. Most important, Kindle makes it more convenient for readers to buy more books. Anytime you make something simpler and lower friction, you get more of it.

We humans coevolve with our tools. We change our tools, and then our tools change us. Writing, invented thousands of years ago, is a grand whopper of a tool, and I have no doubt that it changed us dramatically. Five hundred years ago, Gutenberg's invention led to a significant step-change in the cost of books. Physical books ushered in a new way of collaborating and learning. Lately, networked tools such as desktop computers, laptops, cell phones and PDAs have changed us too. They've shifted us more toward *information snacking*, and I would argue toward shorter attention spans. I value my BlackBerry—I'm convinced it makes me more productive—but I don't want to read a three-hundred-page document on it. Nor do I want to read something hundreds of pages long on my desktop computer or my laptop. As I've already mentioned in this letter, people do more of what's convenient and friction-free. If our tools make information snacking easier, we'll shift more toward information snacking and away from long-form reading. Kindle is purpose-built for long-form reading. We hope Kindle and its successors may gradually and incrementally move us over years into a world with longer spans of attention, providing a counterbalance to the recent proliferation of info-snacking tools. I realize my tone here tends toward the missionary, and I can assure you it's heartfelt. It's also not unique to me but is shared by a large group of folks here. I'm glad about that because missionaries build better products. I'll also point out that, while I'm convinced books are on the verge of being improved upon, Amazon has no sinecure as that agent. It will happen, but if we don't execute well, it will be done by others.

Your team of missionaries here is fervent about driving free cash flow per share and returns on capital. We know we can do that by putting customers first. I guarantee you there is more innovation ahead of us than behind us, and we do not expect the road to be an easy one. We're hopeful, and I'd even say optimistic, that Kindle, true to its name, will "start a fire" and improve the world of reading.

Kindle exemplifies our philosophy and long-term investment approach discussed in our first letter to shareholders in 1997.

Working Backward

2008

IN THIS TURBULENT global economy, our fundamental approach
remains the same. Stay heads down, focused on the long term
and obsessed over customers. Long-term thinking levers our existing abilities and lets us do new things we couldn't otherwise contemplate. It supports the failure and iteration required for invention,
and it frees us to pioneer in unexplored spaces. Seek instant grati-
fication—or the elusive promise of it—and chances are you'll find a
crowd there ahead of you. Long-term orientation interacts well with
customer obsession. If we can identify a customer need and if we
can further develop conviction that that need is meaningful and durable, our approach permits us to work patiently for multiple years
to deliver a solution. "Working backward" from customer needs can
be contrasted with a "skills-forward" approach where existing skills
and competencies are used to drive business opportunities. The
skills-forward approach says, "We are really good at X. What else can
we do with X?" That's a useful and rewarding business approach.
However, if used exclusively, the company employing it will never
be driven to develop fresh skills. Eventually the existing skills will

become outmoded. Working backward from customer needs often *demands* that we acquire new competencies and exercise new muscles, never mind how uncomfortable and awkward-feeling those first steps might be.

Kindle is a good example of our fundamental approach. More than four years ago, we began with a long-term vision: every book, ever printed, in any language, all available in less than sixty seconds. The customer experience we envisioned didn't allow for any hard lines of demarcation between Kindle the device and Kindle the service—the two had to blend together seamlessly. Amazon had never designed or built a hardware device, but rather than change the vision to accommodate our then-existing skills, we hired a number of talented (and missionary!) hardware engineers and got started learning a new institutional skill, one that we needed to better serve readers in the future.

We're grateful and excited that Kindle sales have exceeded our most optimistic expectations. On February 23, we began shipping Kindle 2. If you haven't seen it, Kindle 2 is everything customers loved about the original Kindle, only thinner, faster, with a crisper display, and longer battery life, and capable of holding fifteen hundred books. You can choose from more than 250,000 of the most popular books, magazines, and newspapers. Wireless delivery is free, and you'll have your book in less than sixty seconds. We've received thousands of feedback emails from customers about Kindle, and—remarkably—26 percent of them contain the word "love."

Customer Experience Pillars

In our retail business, we have strong conviction that customers value low prices, vast selection, and fast, convenient delivery and that these needs will remain stable over time. It is difficult for us to imagine that ten years from now, customers will want higher prices, less selection, or slower delivery. Our belief in the durability of these pillars is what gives us the confidence required to invest in strengthening them. We know that the energy we put in now will continue to pay dividends well into the future.

Our pricing objective is to earn customer trust, not to optimize short-term profit dollars. We take it as an article of faith that pricing in this manner is the best way to grow our aggregate profit dollars over the long term. We may make less per item, but by consistently earning trust we will sell many more items. Therefore, we offer low prices across our entire product range. For the same reason, we continue to invest in our free shipping programs, including Amazon Prime. Customers are well informed and smart, and they evaluate the total cost, including delivery charges, when making their purchasing decisions. In the last twelve months, customers worldwide have saved more than $800 million by taking advantage of our free shipping offers.

We're relentlessly focused on adding selection, both by increasing selection inside existing categories and by adding new categories. We've added twenty-eight new categories since 2007. One business that is rapidly growing and continues to surprise me is our shoe store, Endless.com, which we launched in 2007. Fast, reliable delivery is important to customers. In 2005, we launched Amazon Prime. For $79 per year,* Prime members get unlimited express two-day shipping for free and upgrades to one-day delivery for just $3.99. In 2007, we launched Fulfillment by Amazon, a new service for third-party sellers. With FBA, sellers warehouse their inventory in our global fulfillment network, and we pick, pack, and ship to the end customer on the sellers' behalf. FBA items are eligible for Amazon Prime and Super Saver Shipping—just as if the items were Amazon-owned inventory. As a result, FBA both improves the customer experience and drives seller sales. In the fourth quarter of

---

*Prime is a global program: ¥3,900 in Japan, £48 in the United Kingdom, €29 in Germany, and €49 in France.

2008, we shipped more than three million units on behalf of sellers who use Fulfillment by Amazon, a win-win for customers and sellers.

Prudent Spending

The customer-experience path we've chosen requires us to have an efficient cost structure. The good news for shareowners is that we see much opportunity for improvement in that regard. Everywhere we look (and we all look), we find what experienced Japanese manufacturers would call *muda*, or waste.* I find this incredibly energizing. I see it as potential—years and years of variable and fixed productivity gains and more efficient, higher velocity, more flexible capital expenditures.

Our primary financial goal remains maximizing long-term free cash flow and doing so with high rates of return on invested capital. We are investing heartily in Amazon Web Services, in tools for third-party sellers, in digital media, in China, and in new product categories. And we make these investments with the belief that they can be of meaningful scale and can clear our high bar for returns.

Around the world, amazing, inventive, and hard-working Amazonians are putting customers first. I take great pride in being part of this team. We thank you, our owners, for your support, for your encouragement, and for joining us on our continuing adventure.

---

*At a fulfillment center recently, one of our Kaizen experts asked me, "I'm in favor of a clean fulfillment center, but why are you cleaning? Why don't you eliminate the source of dirt?" I felt like the Karate Kid.

Setting Goals

2009

THE FINANCIAL RESULTS for 2009 reflect the cumulative effect of fifteen years of customer experience improvements: increasing selection, speeding delivery, reducing cost structure so we can afford to offer customers ever-lower prices, and many others. This work has been done by a large number of smart, relentless, customer-devoted people across all areas of the company. We are proud of our low prices, our reliable delivery, and our in-stock position on even obscure and hard-to-find items. We also know that we can still be much better, and we're dedicated to improving further.

Some notable highlights from 2009:

Net sales increased 28 percent year-over-year to $24.51 billion in 2009. This is fifteen times higher than net sales ten years ago when they were $1.64 billion in 1999.

Free cash flow increased 114 percent year-over-year to $2.92 billion in 2009.

More customers are taking advantage of Amazon Prime, with worldwide memberships up significantly over last year. The number of different items available for immediate shipment grew more than 50 percent in 2009.

We added twenty-one new product categories around the world in 2009, including Automotive in Japan, Baby in France, and Shoes and Apparel in China.

It was a busy year for our shoes business. In November we acquired Zappos, a leader in online apparel and footwear sales that strives to provide shoppers with the best possible service and selection. Zappos is a terrific addition to our Endless, Javari, Amazon, and Shopbop selection.

The apparel team continued to enhance customer experience with the launch of our Denim Shop offering one hundred brands, including Joe's Jeans, Lucky Brand, 7 For All Mankind, and Levi's.

The shoes and apparel teams created over 121,000 product descriptions and uploaded over 2.2 million images to the website, providing customers with a vivid shopping experience.

Approximately seven million customer reviews were added to websites worldwide.

Sales of products by third-party sellers on our websites represented 30 percent of unit sales in 2009. Active seller accounts increased 24 percent to 1.9 million for the year. Globally, sellers using Fulfillment by Amazon stowed more than one million unique items in our fulfillment center network, thereby making these items available for Free Super Saver Shipping and Amazon Prime.

Amazon Web Services continued its rapid pace of innovation, launching many new services and features, including the Amazon Relational Database Service, Virtual Private Cloud, Elastic MapReduce, High-Memory EC2 Instances, Reserved and Spot Instances, Streaming for Amazon CloudFront, and Versioning for Amazon S3. AWS also continued to expand its global footprint to include additional services in the EU and a new Northern California region and plans for a presence in the Asia-Pacific region in 2010.

The continued innovation and track record for operational performance helped AWS add more customers in 2009 than ever before, including many large enterprise customers.

The US Kindle Store now has more than 460,000 books, an increase from 250,000 last year, and includes 103 of the 110 *New York Times* best sellers, more than 8,900 blogs, and 171 top US and international newspapers and magazines. We have shipped Kindles to more than 120 countries, and we now provide content in six different languages.

Senior leaders that are new to Amazon are often surprised by how little time we spend discussing actual financial results or debating projected financial outputs. To be clear, we take these financial outputs seriously, but we believe that focusing our energy on the controllable inputs to our business is the most effective way to maximize financial outputs over time. Our annual goal setting process begins in the fall and concludes early in the new year after we've completed our peak holiday quarter. Our goal setting sessions are lengthy, spirited, and detail oriented. We have a high bar for the experience our customers deserve and a sense of urgency to improve that experience.

We've been using this same annual process for many years. For 2010, we have 452 detailed goals with owners, deliverables, and targeted completion dates. These are not the only goals our teams set for themselves, but they are the ones we feel are most important to monitor. None of these goals are easy and many will not be achieved without invention. We review the status of each of these goals several times per year among our senior leadership team and add, remove, and modify goals as we proceed.

A review of our current goals reveals some interesting statistics:

360 of the 452 goals will have a direct impact on customer experience.

The word *revenue* is used eight times and *free cash flow* is used only four times.

In the 452 goals, the terms *net income, gross profit* or *margin,* and *operating profit* are not used once.

Taken as a whole, the set of goals is indicative of our fundamental approach. Start with customers and work backward. Listen to customers, but don't *just* listen to customers—also invent on their behalf. We can't assure you that we'll meet all of this year's goals. We haven't in past years. However, we can assure you that we'll continue to obsess over customers. We have strong conviction that that approach—in the long term—is every bit as good for owners as it is for customers.

It's still Day 1.

Fundamental Tools

2010

RANDOM FORESTS, NAIVE Bayesian estimators, RESTful services, gossip protocols, eventual consistency, data sharding, antientropy, Byzantine quorum, erasure coding, vector clocks: walk into certain Amazon meetings, and you may momentarily think you've stumbled into a computer science lecture.

Look inside a current textbook on software architecture, and you'll find few patterns that we don't apply at Amazon. We use high-performance transactions systems, complex rendering and object caching, workflow and queuing systems, business intelligence and data analytics, machine learning and pattern recognition, neural networks and probabilistic decision making, and a wide variety of other techniques. And while many of our systems are based on the latest in computer science research, this often hasn't been sufficient: our architects and engineers have had to advance research in directions that no academic had yet taken. Many of the problems we face have no textbook solutions, and so we—happily—invent new approaches.

Our technologies are almost exclusively implemented as *services*: bits of logic that encapsulate the data they operate on and provide hardened interfaces as the only way to access their functionality. This approach reduces side effects and allows services to evolve at their own pace without impacting the other components of the overall system. Service-oriented architecture—or SOA—is the fundamental building abstraction for Amazon technologies. Thanks to a thoughtful and far-sighted team of engineers and architects, this approach was applied at Amazon long before SOA became a buzzword in the industry. Our e-commerce platform is composed of a federation of hundreds of software services that work in concert to deliver functionality ranging from recommendations to order fulfillment to inventory tracking. For example, to construct a product detail page for a customer visiting Amazon.com, our software calls on between two and three hundred services to present a highly personalized experience for that customer.

State management is the heart of any system that needs to grow to a very large size. Many years ago, Amazon's requirements reached a point where many of our systems could no longer be served by any commercial solution: our key data services store many petabytes of data and handle millions of requests per second. To meet these demanding and unusual requirements, we've developed several alternative, purpose-built persistence solutions, including our own key-value store and single table store. To do so, we've leaned heavily on the core principles from the distributed systems and database research communities and invented from there. The storage systems we've pioneered demonstrate extreme scalability while maintaining tight control over performance, availability, and cost. To achieve their ultra-scale properties these systems take a novel approach to data update management: by relaxing the synchronization requirements of updates that need to be disseminated to large numbers of replicas, these systems are able to survive under the harshest performance and availability conditions. These implementations are based on the concept of eventual consistency. The advances in data management developed by Amazon engineers have been the starting point for the architectures underneath the cloud storage and data management services offered by Amazon Web Services (AWS). For example, our Simple Storage Service, Elastic Block Store, and SimpleDB all derive their basic architecture from unique Amazon technologies.

Other areas of Amazon's business face similarly complex data processing and decision problems, such as product data ingestion and categorization, demand forecasting, inventory allocation, and fraud detection. Rule-based systems can be used successfully, but they can be hard to maintain and can become brittle over time. In many cases, advanced machine learning techniques provide more accurate classification and can self-heal to adapt to changing conditions. For example, our search engine employs data mining and machine learning algorithms that run in the background to build topic models, and we apply information extraction algorithms to identify attributes and extract entities from unstructured descriptions, allowing customers to narrow their searches and quickly find the desired product. We consider a large number of factors in search relevance to predict the probability of a customer's interest and optimize the ranking of results. The diversity of products demands that we employ modern regression techniques like trained random forests of decision trees to flexibly incorporate thousands of product attributes at rank time. The end result of all this behind-the-scenes software? Fast, accurate search results that help you find what you want.

All the effort we put into technology might not matter that much if we kept technology off to the side in some sort of R&D department, but we don't take that approach. Technology infuses all of our teams, all of our processes, our decision making, and our approach to innovation in each of our businesses. It is deeply integrated into everything we do.

One example is Whispersync, our Kindle service designed to ensure that everywhere you go, no matter what devices you have with you, you can access your reading library and all of your highlights, notes, and bookmarks, all in sync across your Kindle devices and mobile apps. The technical challenge is making this a reality for millions of Kindle owners, with hundreds of millions of books, and hundreds of device types, living in over one hundred countries around the world—at 24/7 reliability. At the heart of Whispersync is an eventually consistent replicated data store, with application defined conflict resolution that must and can deal with device isolation lasting weeks or longer. As a Kindle customer, of course, we hide all this technology from you. So when you open your Kindle, it's in sync and on the right page. To paraphrase Arthur C. Clarke, like any sufficiently advanced technology, it's indistinguishable from magic.

Now, if the eyes of some shareowners dutifully reading this letter are by this point glazing over, I will awaken you by pointing out that, in my opinion, these techniques are not idly pursued—they lead directly to free cash flow.

We live in an era of extraordinary increases in available bandwidth, disk space, and processing power, all of which continue to get cheap fast. We have on our team some of the most sophisticated technologists in the world—helping to solve challenges that are right on the edge of what's possible today. As I've discussed many times before, we have unshakeable conviction that the long-term interests of shareowners are perfectly aligned with the interests of customers.

And we like it that way. Invention is in our DNA and technology is the fundamental tool we wield to evolve and improve every aspect of the experience we provide our customers. We still have a lot to learn, and I expect and hope we'll continue to have so much fun learning it. I take great pride in being part of this team.

It's still Day 1.

The Power of Invention

2011

To us, the value of Amazon Web Services is undeniable—in twenty seconds, we can double our server capacity. In a high-growth environment like ours and with a small team of developers, it's very important for us to trust that we have the best support to give to the music community around the world. Five years ago, we would have crashed and been down without knowing when we would be back. Now, because of Amazon's continued innovation, we can provide the best technology and continue to grow." That's Christopher Tholen, the chief technology officer of BandPage. His comments about how AWS helps with the critical need to scale compute capacity quickly and reliably are not hypothetical: BandPage now helps five hundred thousand bands and artists connect with tens of millions of fans.

"So, I started selling on Amazon in April of 2011, and by the time we became the top Amazon lunchbox seller in June, we had between 50 and 75 orders a day. When we hit August and September—our busiest time, with the start of the school year—we had 300, sometimes 500 orders a day. It was just phenomenal. . . . I'm using

Amazon to fulfill my orders, which makes my life easier. Plus, when my customers found out they could get free shipping with Prime subscriptions, the lunchboxes began selling like crazy." Kelly Lester is the "mom entrepreneur" of EasyLunchboxes, her own innovative line of easy-to-pack, environmentally friendly lunchbox containers.

"I sort of stumbled onto it, and it opened a whole new world for me. Since I had over a thousand [book] titles at my house, I thought, 'I'll give this a try.' I sold some and I kept expanding it and expanding it, and come to find out this was so much fun I decided I don't ever want to get another job again. And I've got no boss—other than my wife, that is. What could be better than that? We actually work together on this. We both go out hunting, so it's a team effort that's worked out very well. We sell about 700 books a month. We ship between 800 and 900 to Amazon each month and Amazon ships out the 700 that people buy. Without Amazon handling shipping and customer service, my wife and I would have to be running to the post office or someplace every day with dozens of packages. With that part taken care of for us, life is much simpler. . . . This is a ter- rific program and I love it. After all, Amazon supplies the customers and even ships the books. I mean, how can it get better than that?" Bob Frank founded RJF Books and More after getting laid off in the midst of the economic downturn. He and his wife split their time be- tween Phoenix and Minneapolis, and he describes finding the books he sells like "a treasure hunt every day."

"Because of Kindle Direct Publishing, I earn more royalties in one month than I ever did in a year of writing for a traditional house. I have gone from worrying about if I will be able to pay the bills—and there were many months when I couldn't—to finally having real sav- ings, even thinking about a vacation; something I haven't done in years. . . . Amazon has allowed me to really spread my wings. Prior, I was boxed into a genre, yet I had all of these other books I wanted to write. Now I can do just that. I manage my career. I feel as if I finally have a partner in Amazon. They understand this business and have changed the face of publishing for the good of the writer and the reader, putting choices back into our hands." That's A. K. Alexander, author of *Daddy's Home*, one of the top one hundred best-selling Kindle books in March.

"I had no idea that March of 2010, the first month I decided to publish on KDP, would be a defining moment in my life. Within a year of doing so, I was making enough on a monthly basis to quit my day job and focus on writing full time! The rewards that have sprung out of deciding to publish through KDP have been nothing short of life changing. Financially. Personally. Emotionally. Creatively. The ability to write full time, to be home with my family, and to write exactly what I want without the input of a legacy publisher marketing committee wanting to have a say in every detail of my writing, has made me a stronger writer, a more prolific writer, and most importantly a far happier one. . . . Amazon and KDP are literally enabling creativity in the publishing world and giving writers like me a shot at their dream, and for that I am forever grateful." That's Blake Crouch, author of several thrillers, including the Kindle best seller *Run*.

"Amazon has made it possible for authors like me to get their work in front of readers and has changed my life. In a little over a year, I have sold nearly 250,000 books through the Kindle and have traded in old dreams for bigger and better ones. Four of my books have hit the Top 100 Kindle Best Sellers List. Also, I have been approached by agents, foreign sales people, and two movie producers, and have received mentions in the *LA Times*, *Wall Street Journal*, and *PC Magazine*, and was recently interviewed by *USA Today*. Mostly, I am excited that all writers now have the opportunity to get their work in front of readers without jumping through insurmountable hoops. Writers have more options and readers have more choices. The publishing world is changing fast, and I plan to enjoy every minute of the ride." Theresa Ragan is the KDP author of multiple Kindle best sellers, including *Abducted*.

"Past age 60 and in the midst of the recession, my wife and I found our income options severely limited. KDP was my one shot at a lifelong dream—our only chance at financial salvation. Within months of publishing, KDP has completely changed our lives, enabling this aging nonfiction writer to launch a brand-new career as a best-selling novelist. I can't say enough on behalf of Amazon and the many tools that they make available to independent authors. Without reservation, I urge fellow writers to investigate and seize the opportunities that KDP offers. As I've happily discovered, there is zero downside risk—and the potential is virtually unlimited." Robert Bidinotto is the author of the Kindle best seller *Hunter: A Thriller.*

"I leveraged KDP's technology to blow through all the traditional gatekeepers. Can you imagine how that feels, after struggling so hard, for so long, for every . . . single . . . reader? Now, inspirational fiction lovers I never would have reached are enjoying *Nobody* and my other two novels from the Kindle Store at $2.99. I've always wanted to write a Cinderella story. Now I have. And, thanks to Prince Charming (KDP), there will be more to come . . ." Creston Mapes is the author of the Kindle best seller *Nobody.*

Invention comes in many forms and at many scales. The most radical and transformative of inventions are often those that empower *others* to unleash *their* creativity—to pursue *their* dreams. That's a big part of what's going on with Amazon Web Services, Fulfillment by Amazon, and Kindle Direct Publishing. With AWS, FBA, and KDP, we are creating powerful self-service platforms that allow thousands of people to boldly experiment and accomplish things that would otherwise be impossible or impractical. These innovative, large-scale platforms are not zero-sum—they create win-win situations and create significant value for developers, entrepreneurs, customers, authors, and readers.

Amazon Web Services has grown to have thirty different services and thousands of large and small businesses and individual developers as customers. One of the first AWS offerings, the Simple Storage Service, or S3, now holds over nine hundred billion data objects, with more than a billion new objects being added every day. S3 routinely handles more than five hundred thousand transactions per second and has peaked at close to a million transactions per second. All AWS services are pay-as-you-go and radically transform capital expense into a variable cost. AWS is self-service: you don't need to negotiate a contract or engage with a salesperson—you can just read the online documentation and get started. AWS services are elastic—they easily scale up and easily scale down.

In just the last quarter of 2011, Fulfillment by Amazon shipped tens of millions of items on behalf of sellers. When sellers use FBA, their items become eligible for Amazon Prime, for Super Saver Shipping, and for Amazon returns processing and customer service. FBA is self-service and comes with an easy-to-use inventory management console as part of Amazon Seller Central. For the more technically inclined, it also comes with a set of APIs so that you can use our global fulfillment center network like a giant computer peripheral.

I am emphasizing the self-service nature of these platforms because it's important for a reason I think is somewhat nonobvious: even well-meaning gatekeepers slow innovation. When a platform is self-service, even the improbable ideas can get tried, because there's no expert gatekeeper ready to say, "That will never work!" And guess what—many of those improbable ideas do work, and society is the beneficiary of that diversity.

Kindle Direct Publishing has quickly taken on astonishing scale—more than a thousand KDP authors now each sell more than a thousand copies a month, some have already reached hundreds of thousands of sales, and two have already joined the Kindle Million Club. KDP is a big win for authors. Authors who use KDP get to keep their copyrights, keep their derivative rights, get to publish on their schedule—a typical delay in traditional publishing can be a year or more from the time the book is finished—and, saving the best for last, KDP authors can get paid royalties of 70 percent. The largest traditional publishers pay royalties of only 17.5 percent on ebooks (they pay 25 percent of 70 percent of the selling price, which works out to be 17.5 percent of the selling price). The KDP royalty structure is completely transformative for authors. A typical selling price for a KDP book is a reader-friendly $2.99—authors get approximately $2 of that! With the legacy royalty of 17.5 percent, the selling price would have to be $11.43 to yield the same $2 per unit royalty. I assure you that authors sell many, many more copies at $2.99 than they would at $11.43.

Kindle Direct Publishing is good for readers because they get lower prices, but perhaps just as important, readers also get access to more diversity since authors that might have been rejected by establishment publishing channels now get their chance in the marketplace. You can get a pretty good window into this. Take a look at the Kindle best-seller list, and compare it to the *New York Times* best-seller list—which is more diverse? The Kindle list is chock-full of books from small presses and self-published authors, while the *New York Times* list is dominated by successful and established authors.

Amazonians are leaning into the future, with radical and transformational innovations that create value for thousands of authors, entrepreneurs, and developers. Invention has become second nature at Amazon, and in my view the team's pace of innovation is even accelerating—I can assure you it's very energizing. I'm extremely proud of the whole team and feel lucky to have a front row seat.

It's still Day 1!

Internally Driven

2012

A S REGULAR READERS of this letter will know, our energy at Amazon comes from the desire to impress customers rather than the zeal to best competitors. We don't take a view on which of these approaches is more likely to maximize business success. There are pros and cons to both and many examples of highly successful competitor-focused companies. We do work to pay attention to competitors and be inspired by them, but it is a fact that the customer-centric way is at this point a defining element of our culture.

One advantage—perhaps a somewhat subtle one—of a customer-driven focus is that it aids a certain type of proactivity. When we're at our best, we don't wait for external pressures. We are *internally* driven to improve our services, adding benefits and features, before we have to. We lower prices and increase value for customers before we have to. We invent before we have to. These investments are motivated by customer focus rather than by reaction to competition. We think this approach earns more trust with customers and drives rapid improvements in customer experience—importantly—even in those areas where we are already the leader.

"Thank you. Every time I see that white paper on the front page of Amazon, I know that I'm about to get more for my money than I thought I would. I signed up for Prime for the shipping, yet now I get movies, and TV and books. You keep adding more, but not charging more. So thanks again for the additions." We now have more than fifteen million items in Prime, up fifteen times since we launched in 2005. Prime Instant Video selection tripled in just over a year to more than thirty-eight thousand movies and TV episodes. The Kindle Owners' Lending Library has also more than tripled to over three hundred thousand books, including an investment of millions of dollars to make the entire *Harry Potter* series available as part of that selection. We didn't "have to" make these improvements in Prime. We did so proactively. A related investment—a major, multi-year one—is Fulfillment by Amazon. FBA gives third-party sellers the option of warehousing their inventory alongside ours in our fulfillment center network. It has been a game changer for our seller customers because their items become eligible for Prime benefits, which drives their sales, while at the same time benefitting consumers with additional Prime selection.

We build automated systems that look for occasions when we've provided a customer experience that isn't up to our standards, and those systems then proactively refund customers. One industry observer recently received an automated email from us that said, "We noticed that you experienced poor video playback while watching the following rental on Amazon Video On Demand: Casablanca. We're sorry for the inconvenience and have issued you a refund for the following amount: $2.99. We hope to see you again soon." Surprised by the proactive refund, he ended up writing about the experience: "Amazon 'noticed that I experienced poor video playback . . .' And they decided to give me a refund because of that? Wow . . . Talk about putting customers first."

When you preorder something from Amazon, we guarantee you the lowest price offered by us between your order time and the end of the day of the release date. "I just received notice of a $5 refund to my credit card for pre-order price protection. . . . What a great way to do business! Thank you very much for your fair and honest dealings." Most customers are too busy themselves to monitor the price of an item after they preorder it, and our policy could be to require the customer to contact us and ask for the refund. Doing it proactively is more expensive for us, but it also surprises, delights, and earns trust.

We also have authors as customers. Amazon Publishing has just announced it will start paying authors their royalties monthly, sixty days in arrears. The industry standard is twice a year, and that has been the standard for a long time. Yet when we interview authors as customers, infrequent payment is a major dissatisfier. Imagine how you'd like it if you were paid twice a year. There isn't competitive pressure to pay authors more than once every six months, but we're proactively doing so. By the way—though the research was taxing, I struggled through and am happy to report that I recently saw many Kindles in use at a Florida beach. There are five generations of Kindle, and I believe I saw every generation in use except for the first. Our business approach is to sell premium hardware at roughly breakeven prices. We want to make money when people use our devices—not when people buy our devices. We think this aligns us better with customers. For example, we don't need our customers to be on the upgrade treadmill. We can be very happy to see people still using four-year-old Kindles!

I can keep going—Kindle Fire's FreeTime, our customer service Andon Cord, Amazon MP3's AutoRip—but will finish up with a very clear example of internally driven motivation: Amazon Web Services. In 2012, AWS announced 159 new features and services. We've reduced AWS prices twenty-seven times since launching seven years ago, added enterprise service support enhancements, and created innovative tools to help customers be more efficient. AWS Trusted Advisor monitors customer configurations, compares them to known best practices, and then notifies customers where opportunities exist to improve performance, enhance security, or save money. Yes, we are actively telling customers they're paying us more than they need to. In the last ninety days, customers have saved millions of dollars through Trusted Advisor, and the service is only getting started. All of this progress comes in the context of AWS being the widely recognized leader in its area—a situation where you might worry that external motivation could fail. On the other hand, internal motivation—the drive to get the customer to say "Wow"—keeps the pace of innovation fast.

Our heavy investments in Prime, AWS, Kindle, digital media, and customer experience in general strike some as too generous, shareholder indifferent, or even at odds with being a for-profit company. "Amazon, as far as I can tell, is a charitable organization being run by elements of the investment community for the benefit of consumers," writes one outside observer. But I don't think so. To me, trying to dole out improvements in a just-in-time fashion would be too clever by half. It would be risky in a world as fast-moving as the one we all live in. More fundamentally, I think long-term thinking squares the circle. Proactively delighting customers earns trust, which earns more business from those customers, even in new business arenas. Take a long-term view, and the interests of customers and shareholders align.

As I write this, our recent stock performance has been positive, but we constantly remind ourselves of an important point—as I frequently quote famed investor Benjamin Graham in our employee all-hands meetings—"In the short run, the market is a voting machine but in the long run, it is a weighing machine." We don't celebrate a 10 percent increase in the stock price like we celebrate excellent customer experience. We aren't 10 percent smarter when that happens and conversely aren't 10 percent dumber when the stock goes the other way. We want to be weighed, and we're always working to build a heavier company.

As proud as I am of our progress and our inventions, I know that we will make mistakes along the way—some will be self-inflicted,

"Wow"

2013

I'M SO PROUD of what all the teams here at Amazon have accomplished on behalf of customers this past year. Amazonians around the world are polishing products and services to a degree that is beyond what's expected or required, taking the long view, reinventing normal, and getting customers to say "Wow."

I'd like to take you on a tour that samples a small subset of our various initiatives, ranging from Prime to Amazon Smile to Mayday. The goal is to give you a sense for how much is going on across Amazon and how exciting it is to work on these programs. This broad array of initiatives is only possible because a large team of talented people at every level are exercising their good judgment every day and always asking, how do we make this better?

Ok, let's get started on the tour.

Prime

Customers love Prime. More than one million customers joined Prime in the third week of December alone, and there are now tens of millions of Prime members worldwide. On a per customer basis, Prime members are ordering more items, across more categories, than ever before. Even internally, it's easy for us to forget that Prime was a new, unproven (some even said foolhardy) concept when we launched it nine years ago: all-you-can-eat, two-day shipping for a flat annual fee. At that time, we had one million eligible Prime products. This year, we passed twenty million eligible products, and we continue to add more. We've made Prime better in other ways too, adding new digital benefits—including the Kindle Owners' Lending Library and Prime Instant Video. And we're not done. We have many ideas for how to make Prime even better.

Readers and Authors

We're investing heavily on behalf of readers. The all-new, high-resolution, high-contrast Kindle Paperwhite launched to rave reviews. We integrated the very impressive Goodreads into Kindle, introduced FreeTime for Kindle, and launched Kindle in India, Mexico, and Australia. Bringing joy to air travelers, the FAA approved the use of electronic devices during takeoff and landing. Our public policy team, with the help of many allies, worked patiently for four years on this, at one point loading a test plane with 150 active Kindles. Yes, it all worked fine!

Joining CreateSpace, Kindle Singles, and Kindle Direct Publishing is the new service Kindle Worlds, the literary journal Day One, eight new Amazon Publishing imprints, and the launch of Amazon Publishing in the UK and Germany. Thousands of authors are already using these services to build fulfilling writing careers. Many write and tell us how we have helped them send their children to college, pay off medical bills, or purchase a home. We are missionaries for reading and these stories inspire and encourage us to keep inventing on behalf of writers and readers.

Prime Instant Video

Prime Instant Video is experiencing tremendous growth across all metrics—including new customers, repeat usage, and total number of streams. These are output metrics and they suggest we are on a good path, focusing on the right inputs. Two of the key inputs are the growth of selection and the desirability of that selection. Since we launched PIV in 2011 with five thousand titles, we've grown selection to more than forty thousand movies and TV episodes—all included in your Prime membership. PIV has exclusives on hundreds of sought-after TV seasons including *Downton Abbey*, the ratings blockbuster *Under the Dome, The Americans, Justified, Grimm, Orphan Black*, and kids' programs such as *SpongeBob SquarePants, Dora the Explorer*, and *Blue's Clues*. In addition, our Amazon Studios team continues to invest heavily in original content. Garry Trudeau's *Alpha House*, starring John Goodman, debuted last year and quickly became the most-watched show on Amazon. We recently greenlit six more originals, including *Bosch*, by Michael Connelly, *The After*, from Chris Carter of *The X-Files*, *Mozart in the Jungle*, from Roman Coppola and Jason Schwartzman, and Jill Soloway's beautiful *Transparent*, which some have called the best pilot in years. We like our approach and are replicating it with our recent rollout of PIV in both the UK and Germany. The early customer response in those countries has been terrific, surpassing our expectations.

Fire TV

Just this past week, after two years of hard work, our hardware team launched Fire TV. Not only is Fire TV the best way to watch Amazon's video offerings, it also embraces non-Amazon content services like Netflix, Hulu Plus, VEVO, WatchESPN, and many more. Fire TV has big hardware specs in a category that's previously been hardware-light. It shows. Fire TV is fast and fluid. And our ASAP technology predicts what you might want to watch and prebuffers it, so shows start instantly. Our team also put a small microphone in the remote control. Hold down the mic button on the remote, and you can speak your search term rather than type it into an alphabet grid. The team has done a terrific job—the voice search actually works.

In addition to Prime Instant Video, Fire TV gives you instant access to over two hundred thousand movies and TV episodes available a la carte, including new releases like *Gravity, 12 Years a Slave, Dallas Buyers Club, Frozen,* and more. As a bonus, Fire TV also lets you play high-quality, inexpensive games on your living room TV. We hope you try it out. If you do, let us know what you think. The team would love to hear your feedback.

Amazon Game Studios

It's early in the twenty-second century and Earth is threatened by an alien species, the Ne'ahtu. The aliens infected Earth's energy grid with a computer virus to disable the planet's defenses.

Before they could strike, computer science prodigy Amy Ramanujan neutralized the alien virus and saved the planet. Now, the Ne'ahtu are back and Dr. Ramanujan must prevent them from launching an all-out invasion on Earth. She needs your help.

That's how *Sev Zero*, the first Fire TV exclusive from Amazon Game Studios, begins. The team combined tower defense with shooter gameplay and created a co-op mode where one player leads on the ground with their gamepad controller while a second player provides air support from a tablet. I can assure you that there are some intense moments when you'll appreciate a well-timed air-strike. When you see it, you may be surprised that this level of game play is possible on an inexpensive streaming media device. *Sev Zero* is only the first of a collection of innovative and graphically beautiful games we're building from the ground up for Fire tablets and Fire TV.

Amazon Appstore

The Amazon Appstore now serves customers in almost two hundred countries. Selection has grown to include over two hundred thousand apps and games from top developers around the globe—nearly tripling in size over the past year. We introduced Amazon Coins, a virtual currency that saves customers up to 10 percent on app and in-app purchases. Our Whispersync for Games technology lets you start a game on one device and continue it on another without losing your progress. Developers can use the Mobile Associates program to offer millions of physical products from Amazon inside their apps and earn referral fees when customers buy those items. We introduced Appstore Developer Select, a marketing program that promotes new apps and games on Kindle Fire tablets and on Amazon's Mobile Ad Network. We created Analytics and A/B Testing services—free services that empower developers to track user engagement and optimize their apps for iOS, Android, and Fire OS. Also this year, we embraced HTML5 web app developers. They too can now offer their apps on Kindle Fire and through the Amazon Appstore.

Spoken Word Audio

2013 was a landmark year for Audible, the world's largest seller and producer of audiobooks. Audible makes it possible for you to read when your eyes are busy. Millions of customers download hundreds of millions of audiobooks and other spoken-word programming from Audible. Audible customers downloaded close to six hundred million listening hours in 2013. Thanks to Audible Studios, people drive to work listening to Kate Winslet, Colin Firth, Anne Hathaway, and many other stars. One big hit in 2013 was Jake Gyllenhaal's performance of *The Great Gatsby*, which has already sold one hundred thousand copies. Whispersync for Voice allows customers to switch seamlessly back and forth between reading a book on their Kindle and listening to the corresponding Audible book on their smart phone. The *Wall Street Journal* called Whispersync for Voice "Amazon's new killer app for books." If you haven't already, I recommend you give it a try—it's fun and expands the amount of time you have available to read.

Fresh Grocery

After trialing the service for five years in Seattle (no one accuses us of a lack of patience), we expanded Amazon Fresh to Los Angeles and San Francisco. Prime Fresh members pay $299 a year and receive same-day and early morning delivery not only on fresh grocery items but also on over five hundred thousand other items ranging from toys to electronics to household goods. We're also partnering with favorite local merchants (the Cheese Store of Beverly Hills, Pike Place Fish Market, San Francisco Wine Trading Company, and many more) to provide the same convenient home delivery on a great selection of prepared foods and specialty items. We'll continue our methodical approach—measuring and refining Amazon Fresh—with the goal of bringing this incredible service to more cities over time.

Amazon Web Services

AWS is eight years old, and the team's pace of innovation is actually accelerating. In 2010, we launched 61 significant services and features. In 2011, that number was 82. In 2012, it was 159. In 2013:

280. We're also expanding our geographic footprint. We now have ten AWS regions around the world, including the East Coast of the United States, two on the West Coast, Europe, Singapore, Tokyo, Sydney, Brazil, China, and a government-only region called Gov-Cloud. We have twenty-six availability zones across regions and fifty-one edge locations for our content distribution network. The development teams work directly with customers and are empowered to design, build, and launch based on what they learn. We iterate continuously, and when a feature or enhancement is ready, we push it out and make it instantly available to all. This approach is fast, customer-centric, and efficient—it's allowed us to reduce prices more than forty times in the past eight years—and the teams have no plans to slow down.

Employee Empowerment

We challenge ourselves to not only invent outward facing features, but also to find better ways to do things internally—things that will both make us more effective and benefit our thousands of employees around the world.

Career Choice is a program where we prepay 95 percent of tuition for our employees to take courses for in-demand fields, such as airplane mechanic or nursing, regardless of whether the skills are relevant to a career at Amazon. The goal is to enable choice. We know that for some of our fulfillment center employees, Amazon will be a career. For others, Amazon might be a stepping-stone on the way to a job somewhere else—a job that may require new skills. If the right training can make the difference, we want to help.

The second program is called Pay to Quit. It was invented by the clever people at Zappos, and the Amazon fulfillment centers have been iterating on it. Pay to Quit is pretty simple. Once a year, we offer to pay our associates to quit. The first year the offer is made, it's for $2,000. Then it goes up $1,000 a year until it reaches $5,000.

The headline on the offer is "Please Don't Take This Offer." We hope they don't take the offer; we want them to stay. Why do we make this offer? The goal is to encourage folks to take a moment and think about what they really want. In the long run, an employee staying somewhere they don't want to be isn't healthy for the employee or the company.

A third inward innovation is our Virtual Contact Center. It's an idea we started a few years back and have continued to grow with terrific results. Under this program, employees provide customer service support for Amazon and Kindle customers while working from home. This flexibility is ideal for many employees who, perhaps because they have young children or for another reason, either cannot or prefer not to work outside the home. Our Virtual Contact Center is our fastest growing "site" in the United States, operating in more than ten states today. This growth will continue as we hope to double our state footprint in 2014.

Veteran Hiring

We seek leaders who can invent, think big, have a bias for action, and deliver results on behalf of customers. These principles look familiar to men and women who've served our country in the armed forces, and we find that their experience leading people is invaluable in our fast-paced work environment. We're a member of Joining Forces and the 100,000 Jobs Mission—two national efforts that encourage businesses to offer service members and their families career opportunities and support. Our Military Talent team attended more than fifty recruiting events last year to help veterans find job opportunities at Amazon. In 2013, we hired more than nineteen hundred veterans. And once veterans join our team, we offer several programs that help them transition more easily into the civilian workforce and that connect them with our internal network of veterans for mentoring and support. These programs have earned us recognition as a top employer by *G.I. Jobs Magazine, U.S. Veterans Magazine,* and *Military Spouse Magazine,* and we'll continue to invest in military veteran hiring as we grow.

Fulfillment Innovation

Nineteen years ago, I drove the Amazon packages to the post office every evening in the back of my Chevy Blazer. My vision extended so far that I dreamed we might one day get a forklift. Fast-forward to today and we have ninety-six fulfillment centers and are on our seventh generation of fulfillment center design. Our operations team is extraordinary—methodical and ingenious. Through our Kaizen program, named for the Japanese term meaning "change for the better," employees work in small teams to streamline processes and reduce defects and waste. Our Earth Kaizens set energy reduction, recycling, and other green goals. In 2013, more than forty-seven hundred associates participated in eleven hundred Kaizens.

Sophisticated software is key in our FCs. This year, we rolled out 280 major software improvements across the FC network. Our goal is to continue to iterate and improve on the design, layout, technology, and operations in these buildings, ensuring that each new facility we build is better than the last. I invite you to come see one for yourself. We offer fulfillment center tours open to the public, ages six and above. You can find info on the available tours at www.amazon.com/fctours. I'm always amazed when I visit one of our FCs, and I hope you'll arrange a tour. I think you'll be impressed.

Urban Campus

In 2013, we added 420,000 square feet of new headquarters space in Seattle and broke ground on what will become four city blocks and several million square feet of new construction. It is a fact that we could have saved money by instead building in the suburbs, but for us, it was important to stay in the city. Urban campuses are much greener. Our employees are able to take advantage of existing communities and public transit infrastructure, with less dependence on cars. We're investing in dedicated bike lanes to provide safe, pollution-free, easy access to our offices. Many of our employees can live nearby, skip the commute altogether, and walk to work. Though I can't prove it, I also believe an urban headquarters will help keep Amazon vibrant, attract the right talent, and be great for the health and well-being of our employees and the city of Seattle.

Fast Delivery

In partnership with the United States Postal Service, we've begun for the first time to offer Sunday delivery to select cities. Sunday delivery is a win for Amazon customers, and we plan to roll it out to a large portion of the US population throughout 2014. We've created our own fast, last-mile delivery networks in the United Kingdom where commercial carriers couldn't support our peak volumes. In India and China, where delivery infrastructure isn't yet mature, you can see Amazon bike couriers delivering packages throughout the major cities. And there is more invention to come. The Prime Air team is already flight testing our fifth and sixth generation aerial vehicles, and we are in the design phase on generations seven and eight.

Experiments and More Experiments

We have our own internal experimentation platform called "Weblab" that we use to evaluate improvements to our websites and products. In 2013, we ran 1,976 Weblabs worldwide, up from 1,092 in 2012, and 546 in 2011. One recent success is our new feature called "Ask an Owner." It was many years ago that we pioneered the idea of online customer reviews—customers sharing their opinion on a product to help other customers make an informed purchase decision. "Ask" is in that same tradition. From a product page, customers can ask any question related to the product. *Is the product compatible with my TV/Stereo/PC? Is it easy to assemble? How long does the battery last?* We then route these questions to *owners* of the product. As is the case with reviews, customers are happy to share their knowledge to directly help other customers. Millions of questions have already been asked and answered.

Apparel and Shoes

Amazon Fashion is booming. Premium brands are recognizing that they can use Amazon to reach fashion-conscious, high-demo customers, and customers are enjoying the selection, free returns, detailed photos, and video clips that let them see how clothes move and drape as the models walk and turn. We opened a new forty-thousand-square-foot photo studio in Brooklyn and now shoot an average of 10,413 photos every day in the studio's twenty-eight bays. To celebrate the opening, we hosted a design contest with students from Pratt, Parsons, School of Visual Arts, and the Fashion Institute of Technology that was judged by a panel of industry leaders including Steven Kolb, Eva Chen, Derek Lam, Tracy Reese, and Steven Alan. Kudos to Parsons who took home the top prize.

Frustration-Free Packaging

Our battle against annoying wire ties and plastic clamshells rages on. An initiative that began five years ago with a simple idea that you shouldn't have to risk bodily injury opening your new electronics or toys has now grown to over two hundred thousand products, all available in easy-to-open, recyclable packaging designed to alleviate "wrap rage" and help the planet by reducing packaging waste.

We have over two thousand manufacturers in our Frustration-Free Packaging program, including Fisher-Price, Mattel, Unilever, Belkin, Victorinox Swiss Army, Logitech, and many more. We've now shipped many millions of Frustration-Free items to 175 countries. We are also reducing waste for customers—eliminating thirty-three million pounds of excess packaging to date. This program is a perfect example of a missionary team staying heads-down focused on serving customers. Through hard work and perseverance, an idea that started with only nineteen products is now available on hundreds of thousands and benefiting millions of customers.

Fulfillment by Amazon

The number of sellers using Fulfillment by Amazon grew more than 65 percent last year. Growth like that at such large scale is unusual. FBA is unique in many ways. It's not often you get to delight two customer sets with one program. With FBA, sellers can store their products in our fulfillment centers, and we pick, pack, ship, and provide customer service for these products. Sellers benefit from one of the most advanced fulfillment networks in the world, easily scaling their businesses to reach millions of customers. And not just any customers—Prime members. FBA products can be eligible for Prime free two-day shipping. Customers benefit from this additional selection—they get even more value out of their Prime membership. And, unsurprisingly, sellers see increased sales when they join FBA. In a 2013 survey, nearly three out of four FBA respondents reported that their unit sales increased on Amazon.com more than 20 percent after joining FBA. It's a win-win.

> "FBA is the best employee I have ever had. . . . One morning I woke up and realized FBA had shipped 50 units. As soon as I realized I could sell products while I sleep, it was a no-brainer."
> —*Thanny Schuck, Action Sports LLC*

"Starting out as an unknown brand, it was difficult to find retailers willing to stock our goods. No such barriers existed at Amazon. The beauty of Amazon is that someone can say, 'I want to start a business,' and they can go on Amazon and really start a business. You don't have to get a lease on a building or even have any employees at first. You can just do it on your own. And that's what I did."

—Wendell Morris, YogaRat

Login and Pay with Amazon

For several years we've enabled Amazon customers to pay on other sites, such as Kickstarter, SmugMug, and Gogo Inflight, using the credit cards and shipping addresses already stored in their Amazon account. This year, we expanded that capability so customers can also sign in using their Amazon account credentials, saving them the annoyance of needing to remember yet another account name and password. It's convenient for the customer and a business builder for the merchant. Cymax Stores, the online furniture retailer, has seen tremendous success with Login and Pay. It now accounts for 20 percent of their orders, tripling their new account registrations, and increasing purchase conversion 3.15 percent in the first three months. This example isn't unusual. We are seeing results like these with many partners, and the team is excited and encouraged. You should look for more in 2014.

Amazon Smile

In 2013 we launched Amazon Smile—a simple way for customers to support their favorite charitable organizations every time they shop. When you shop at smile.amazon.com, Amazon donates a portion of the purchase price to the charity of your choice. You'll find the same selection, prices, shipping options, and Prime eligibility on smile. amazon.com as you do on Amazon.com—you'll even find your same shopping cart and wish lists. In addition to the large, national charities you would expect, you can also designate your local children's hospital, your school's PTA, or practically any other cause you might like. There are almost a million charities to choose from. I hope you'll find your favorite on the list.

The Mayday Button

"Not only is the device awesome but the Mayday feature is absolutely FANTASTIC!!!!! The Kindle team has hit it out of the park with this one."

"Just tried the mayday button on my hdx. 15 second response time . . . amazon has done it again. Thoroughly impressed."

Nothing gives us more pleasure at Amazon than "reinventing normal"—creating inventions that customers love and resetting their expectations for what normal should be. Mayday reimagines and revolutionizes the idea of on-device tech support. Tap the Mayday button, and an Amazon expert will appear on your Fire HDX and can co-pilot you through any feature by drawing on your screen, walking you through how to do something yourself, or doing it for you—whatever works best. Mayday is available 24/7, 365 days a year, and our response time goal is fifteen seconds or less. We beat that goal—with an average response time of only nine seconds on our busiest day, Christmas.

A few of the Maydays have been amusing. Mayday Tech Advisors have received thirty-five marriage proposals from customers. 475 customers have asked to talk to Amy, our Mayday television personality. 109 Maydays have been customers asking for assistance with ordering a pizza. By a slim margin, Pizza Hut wins customer preference over Domino's. There are forty-four instances where the Mayday Tech Advisor has sung Happy Birthday to the customer. Mayday Tech Advisors have been serenaded by customers 648 times. And three customers have asked for a bedtime story. Pretty cool.

I hope that gives you some sense of the scope of our opportunity and initiatives, as well as the inventive spirit and push for exceptional quality with which they're undertaken. I should underscore again that this is a subset. There are many programs I've omitted in this letter that are just as promising, consequential, and interesting as those I've highlighted.

We have the good fortune of a large, inventive team and a patient, pioneering, customer-obsessed culture—great innovations, large and small, are happening every day on behalf of customers, and at all levels throughout the company. This decentralized distribution of invention throughout the company—not limited to the company's senior leaders—is the only way to get robust, high-throughput innovation. What we're doing is challenging and fun—we get to work in the future. Failure comes part and parcel with invention. It's not optional. We understand that and believe in failing early and iterating until we get it right. When this process works, it means our failures are relatively small in size (most experiments can start small), and when we hit on something that is really working for customers, we double-down on it with hopes to turn it into an even bigger success. However, it's not always as clean as that. Inventing is messy, and over time, it's certain that we'll fail at some big bets too.

I'd like to close by remembering Joy Covey. Joy was Amazon's CFO in the early days, and she left an indelible mark on the company. Joy was brilliant, intense, and so fun. She smiled a lot and her eyes were always wide, missing nothing. She was substance over optics. She was a long-term thinker. She had a deep keel. Joy was bold. She had a profound impact on all of us on the senior team and on the company's entire culture. Part of her will always be here, making sure we watch the details, see the world around us, and all have fun.

I feel super lucky to be a part of the Amazon team. It's still Day 1.

Three Big Ideas

2014

A DREAMY BUSINESS OFFERING has at least four characteristics. Customers love it, it can grow to very large size, it has strong returns on capital, and it's durable in time—with the potential to endure for decades. When you find one of these, don't just swipe right, get married.

Well, I'm pleased to report that Amazon hasn't been monogamous in this regard. After two decades of risk taking and teamwork, and with generous helpings of good fortune all along the way, we are now happily wed to what I believe are three such life partners: Marketplace, Prime, and AWS. Each of these offerings was a bold bet at first, and sensible people worried (often!) that they could not work. But at this point, it's become pretty clear how special they are and how lucky we are to have them. It's also clear that there are no sinecures in business. We know it's our job to always nourish and fortify them.

We'll approach the job with our usual tools: customer obsession rather than competitor focus, heartfelt passion for invention, commitment to operational excellence, and a willingness to think long-term. With good execution and a bit of continuing good luck, Marketplace, Prime, and AWS can be serving customers and earning financial returns for many years to come.

Marketplace

Marketplace's early days were not easy. First, we launched Amazon Auctions. I think seven people came, if you count my parents and siblings. Auctions transformed into zShops, which was basically a fixed price version of Auctions. Again, no customers. But then we morphed zShops into Marketplace. Internally, Marketplace was known as SDP for Single Detail Page. The idea was to take our most valuable retail real estate—our product detail pages—and let third-party sellers compete against our own retail category managers. It was more convenient for customers, and within a year, it accounted for 5 percent of units. Today, more than 40 percent of our units are sold by more than two million third-party sellers worldwide. Customers ordered more than two billion units from sellers in 2014.

The success of this hybrid model accelerated the Amazon flywheel. Customers were initially drawn by our fast-growing selection of Amazon-sold products at great prices with a great customer experience. By then allowing third parties to offer products side by side, we became more attractive to customers, which drew even more sellers. This also added to our economies of scale, which we passed along by lowering prices and eliminating shipping fees for qualifying orders. Having introduced these programs in the United States, we rolled them out as quickly as we could to our other geographies. The result was a marketplace that became seamlessly integrated with all of our global websites.

We work hard to reduce the workload for sellers and increase the success of their businesses. Through our Selling Coach program, we generate a steady stream of automated machine-learned "nudges" (more than seventy million in a typical week)—alerting sellers about opportunities to avoid going out of stock, add selection that's selling, and sharpen their prices to be more competitive. These nudges translate to billions in increased sales to sellers.

To further globalize Marketplace, we're now helping sellers in each of our geographies—and in countries where we don't have a presence—reach out to our customers in countries outside their home geographies. We hosted merchants from more than 100 different countries last year and helped them connect with customers in 185 nations.

Almost one-fifth of our overall third-party sales now occur outside the sellers' home countries, and our merchants' cross-border sales nearly doubled last year. In the EU, sellers can open a single account, manage their business in multiple languages, and make products available across our five EU websites. More recently, we've started consolidating cross-border shipments for sellers and helping them obtain ocean shipping from Asia to Europe and North America at preferential, bulk rates.

Marketplace is the heart of our fast-growing operations in India, since all of our selection in India is offered by third-party sellers. Amazon.in now offers more selection than any other e-commerce site in India—with more than twenty million products offered from over twenty-one thousand sellers. With our Easy Ship service, we pick up products from a seller and handle delivery all the way to the end customer. Building upon Easy Ship, the India team recently piloted Kirana Now, a service that delivers everyday essentials from local kirana (mom and pop) stores to customers in two to four hours, adding convenience for our customers and increasing sales for the stores participating in the service.

Perhaps most important for sellers, we've created Fulfillment by Amazon. But I'll save that for after we discuss Prime.

Amazon Prime

Ten years ago, we launched Amazon Prime, originally designed as an all-you-can-eat free and fast shipping program. We were told repeatedly that it was a risky move, and in some ways it was. In its first year, we gave up many millions of dollars in shipping revenue, and there was no simple math to show that it would be worth it. Our decision to go ahead was built on the positive results we'd seen earlier when we introduced Free Super Saver Shipping, and an intuition that customers would quickly grasp that they were being offered the best deal in the history of shopping. In addition, analysis told us that, if we achieved scale, we would be able to significantly lower the cost of fast shipping.

Our owned-inventory retail business was the foundation of Prime. In addition to creating retail teams to build each of our category-specific online "stores," we have created large-scale systems to automate much of inventory replenishment, inventory placement, and product pricing. The precise delivery-date promise of Prime required operating our fulfillment centers in a new way, and pulling all of this together is one of the great accomplishments of our global operations team. Our worldwide network of fulfillment centers has expanded from 13 in 2005, when we launched Prime, to 109 this year. We are now on our eighth generation of fulfillment center design, employing proprietary software to manage receipt, stowing, picking, and shipment. Amazon Robotics, which began with our acquisition of Kiva in 2012, has now deployed more than fifteen thousand robots to support the stowing and retrieval of products at a higher density and lower cost than ever before. Our owned-inventory retail business remains our best customer-acquisition vehicle for Prime and a critical part of building out categories that attract traffic and third-party sellers.

Though fast delivery remains a core Prime benefit, we are finding new ways to pump energy into Prime. Two of the most important are digital and devices.

In 2011 we added Prime Instant Video as a benefit, now with tens of thousands of movies and TV episodes available for unlimited streaming in the United States, and we've started expanding the program into the United Kingdom and Germany as well. We're investing a significant amount on this content, and it's important that we monitor its impact. We ask ourselves, is it worth it? Is it driving Prime? Among other things, we watch Prime free-trial starts, conversion to paid membership, renewal rates, and product purchase rates by members entering through this channel. We like what we see so far and plan to keep investing here.

While most of our PIV spend is on licensed content, we're also starting to develop original content. The team is off to a strong start. Our show *Transparent* became the first from a streaming service to win a Golden Globe for best series and *Tumble Leaf* won the Annie for best animated series for preschoolers. In addition to the critical acclaim, the numbers are promising. An advantage of our original programming is that its first run is on Prime—it hasn't already appeared anywhere else. Together with the quality of the shows, that first run status appears to be one of the factors leading to the attractive numbers. We also like the fixed cost nature of original programming. We get to spread that fixed cost across our large membership base. Finally, our business model for original content is unique. I'm pretty sure we're the first company to have figured out how to make winning a Golden Globe pay off in increased sales of power tools and baby wipes!

Amazon designed and manufactured devices—from Kindle to Fire TV to Echo—also pump energy into Prime services such as Prime Instant Video and Prime Music, and generally drive higher engagement with every element of the Amazon ecosystem. And there's more to come—our device team has a strong and exciting roadmap ahead.

Prime isn't done improving on its original fast and free shipping promise either. The recently launched Prime Now offers Prime members free two-hour delivery on tens of thousands of items or one-hour delivery for a $7.99 fee. Lots of early reviews read like this one, "In the past six weeks my husband and I have made an embarrassing number of orders through Amazon Prime Now. It's cheap, easy, and insanely fast." We've launched in Manhattan, Brooklyn, Miami, Baltimore, Dallas, Atlanta, and Austin, and more cities are coming soon.

Now, I'd like to talk about Fulfillment by Amazon. FBA is so important because it is the glue that inextricably links Marketplace and Prime. Thanks to FBA, Marketplace and Prime are no longer two things. In fact, at this point, I can't really think about them separately. Their economics and customer experiences are now happily and deeply intertwined.

FBA is a service for Marketplace sellers. When a seller decides to use FBA, they stow their inventory in our fulfillment centers. We take on all logistics, customer service, and product returns. If a customer orders an FBA item and an Amazon owned-inventory item, we can ship both items to the customer in one box—a huge efficiency gain. But even more important, when a seller joins FBA, their items can become Prime eligible.

Maintaining a firm grasp of the obvious is more difficult than one would think it should be. But it's useful to try. If you ask, what do sellers want? The correct (and obvious) answer is: they want more sales. So, what happens when sellers join FBA and their items become Prime eligible? They get more sales.

Notice also what happens from a Prime member's point of view. Every time a seller joins FBA, Prime members get more Prime eligible selection. The value of membership goes up. This is powerful for our flywheel. FBA completes the circle: Marketplace pumps energy into Prime, and Prime pumps energy into Marketplace.

In a 2014 survey of US sellers, 71 percent of FBA merchants reported more than a 20 percent increase in unit sales after joining

FBA. In the holiday period, worldwide FBA units shipped grew 50 percent over the prior year and represented more than 40 percent of paid third-party units. Paid Prime memberships grew more than 50 percent in the United States last year and 53 percent worldwide. FBA is a win for customers and a win for sellers.

Amazon Web Services

A radical idea when it was launched nine years ago, Amazon Web Services is now big and growing fast. Start-ups were the early adopters. On-demand, pay-as-you-go cloud storage and compute resources dramatically increased the speed of starting a new business. Companies like Pinterest, Dropbox, and Airbnb all used AWS services and remain customers today.

Since then, large enterprises have been coming on board as well, and they're choosing to use AWS for the same primary reason the start-ups did: speed and agility. Having lower IT cost is attractive, and sometimes the absolute cost savings can be enormous. But cost savings alone could never overcome deficiencies in performance or functionality. Enterprises are dependent on IT—it's mission critical. So, the proposition, "I can save you a significant amount on your annual IT bill and my service is almost as good as what you have now," won't get too many customers. What customers really want in this arena is "better and faster," and if "better and faster" can come with a side dish of cost savings, terrific. But the cost savings is the gravy, not the steak.

IT is so high leverage. You don't want to imagine a competitor whose IT department is nimbler than yours. Every company has a list of technology projects that the business would like to see implemented as soon as possible. The painful reality is that tough triage decisions are always made, and many projects never get done. Even those that get resourced are often delivered late or with incomplete functionality. If an IT department can figure out how to deliver a larger number of business-enabling technology projects faster, they'll be creating significant and real value for their organization.

These are the main reasons AWS is growing so quickly. IT departments are recognizing that when they adopt AWS, they get more done. They spend less time on low value-add activities like managing datacenters, networking, operating system patches, capacity planning, database scaling, and so on and so on. Just as important, they get access to powerful APIs and tools that dramatically simplify building scalable, secure, robust, high-performance systems. And those APIs and tools are continuously and seamlessly upgraded behind the scenes, without customer effort.

Today, AWS has more than a million active customers as companies and organizations of all sizes use AWS in every imaginable business segment. AWS usage grew by approximately 90 percent in the fourth quarter of 2014 versus the prior year. Companies like GE, Major League Baseball, Tata Motors, and Qantas are building new applications on AWS—these range from apps for crowdsourcing and personalized health care to mobile apps for managing fleets of trucks. Other customers, like NTT DOCOMO, the *Financial Times*, and the Securities and Exchange Commission are using AWS to analyze and take action on vast amounts of data. And many customers like Condé Nast, Kellogg's, and News Corp are migrating legacy critical applications and, in some cases, entire datacenters to AWS.

We've increased our pace of innovation as we've gone along—from nearly 160 new features and services in 2012, to 280 in 2013, and 516 last year. There are many that would be interesting to talk about—from WorkDocs and WorkMail to AWS Lambda and the EC2 Container Service to the AWS Marketplace—but for purposes of brevity, I'm going to limit myself to one: our recently introduced Amazon Aurora. We hope Aurora will offer customers a new normal for a very important (but also very problematic) technology that is a critical underpinning of many applications: the relational database. Aurora is a MySQL-compatible database engine that offers the speed and availability of high-end commercial databases with the simplicity and cost effectiveness of open source databases. Aurora's performance is up to five times better than typical MySQL databases, at one-tenth the cost of commercial database packages. Relational databases is an arena that's been a pain point for organizations and developers for a long time, and we're very excited about Aurora.

I believe AWS is one of those dreamy business offerings that can be serving customers and earning financial returns for many years into the future. Why am I optimistic? For one thing, the size of the opportunity is big, ultimately encompassing global spend on servers, networking, datacenters, infrastructure software, databases, data warehouses, and more. Similar to the way I think about Amazon retail, for all practical purposes, I believe AWS is market-size unconstrained.

Second, its current leadership position (which is significant) is a strong ongoing advantage. We work hard—very hard—to make AWS as easy to use as possible. Even so, it's still a necessarily complex set of tools with rich functionality and a nontrivial learning curve. Once you've become proficient at building complex systems with AWS, you do not want to have to learn a new set of tools and APIs assuming the set you already understand works for you. This is in no way something we can rest on, but if we continue to serve our customers in a truly outstanding way, they will have a rational preference to stick with us.

In addition, also because of our leadership position, we now have thousands of what are effectively AWS ambassadors roaming the world. Software developers changing jobs, moving from one company to another, become our best salespeople: "We used AWS where I used to work, and we should consider it here. I think we'd get more done." It's a good sign that proficiency with AWS and its services is already something software developers are adding to their resumes.

Finally, I'm optimistic that AWS will have strong returns on capital. This is one we as a team examine because AWS is capital intensive. The good news is we like what we see when we do these analyses. Structurally, AWS is far less capital intensive than the mode it's replacing—do-it-yourself datacenters—which have low utilization rates, almost always below 20 percent. Pooling of workloads across customers gives AWS much higher utilization rates, and correspondingly higher capital efficiency. Further, once again our leadership position helps: scale economies can provide us a relative advantage on capital efficiency. We'll continue to watch and shape the business for good returns on capital.

AWS is young, and it is still growing and evolving. We think we can continue to lead if we continue to execute with our customers' needs foremost in mind.

Career Choice

Before closing, I want to take a moment to update shareowners on something we're excited about and proud of. Three years ago we launched an innovative employee benefit—the Career Choice program, where we prepay 95 percent of tuition for employees to take courses for in-demand fields, such as airplane mechanic or nursing, regardless of whether the skills are relevant to a career at Amazon. The idea was simple: enable choice.

We know that, for some of our fulfillment and customer service center employees, Amazon will be a career. For others, Amazon might be a stepping-stone on the way to a job somewhere else—a job that may require new skills. If the right training can make the difference, we want to help, and so far we have been able to help over two thousand employees who have participated in the program in eight different countries. There's been so much interest that we are now building onsite classrooms so college and technical classes can be taught inside our fulfillment centers, making it even easier for associates to achieve these goals.

There are now eight FCs offering fifteen classes taught onsite in our purpose-built classrooms with high-end technology features and designed with glass walls to inspire others to participate and generate encouragement from peers. We believe Career Choice is an innovative way to draw great talent to serve customers in our fulfillment and customer service centers. These jobs can become gateways to great careers with Amazon as we expand around the world or enable employees the opportunity to follow their passion in other in-demand technical fields, like our very first Career Choice graduate did when she started a new career as a nurse in her community.

I would also like to invite you to come join the more than twenty-four thousand people who have signed up so far to see the magic that happens after you click buy on Amazon.com by touring one of our fulfillment centers. In addition to US tours, we are now offering tours at sites around the world, including Rugeley in the United Kingdom and Graben in Germany and continuing to expand. You can sign up for a tour at www.amazon.com/fctours.

Marketplace, Prime, and Amazon Web Services are three big ideas. We're lucky to have them, and we're determined to improve and nurture them—make them even better for customers. You can also count on us to work hard to find a fourth. We've already got a number of candidates in the works, and as we promised some twenty years ago, we'll continue to make bold bets. With the opportunities unfolding in front of us to serve customers better through invention, we assure you we won't stop trying.

It's still Day 1.

Big Winners Pay for
Many Experiments

2015

THIS YEAR, AMAZON became the fastest company ever to reach $100 billion in annual sales. Also this year, Amazon Web Services is reaching $10 billion in annual sales—doing so at a pace even faster than Amazon achieved that milestone.

What's going on here? Both were planted as tiny seeds and both have grown organically without significant acquisitions into meaningful and large businesses, quickly. Superficially, the two could hardly be more different. One serves consumers and the other serves enterprises. One is famous for brown boxes and the other for APIs. Is it only a coincidence that two such dissimilar offerings grew so quickly under one roof? Luck plays an outsized role in every endeavor, and I can assure you we've had a bountiful supply. But beyond that, there is a connection between these two businesses. Under the surface, the two are not so different after all. They share a distinctive organizational culture that cares deeply about and acts with conviction on a small number of principles. I'm talking about customer obsession rather than competitor obsession, eagerness to invent and pioneer, willingness to fail, the patience to think long-term, and the taking of professional pride in operational excellence. Through that lens, AWS and Amazon retail are very similar indeed.

A word about corporate cultures: for better or for worse, they are enduring, stable, hard to change. They can be a source of advantage or disadvantage. You can write down your corporate culture, but when you do so, you're discovering it, uncovering it—not creating it. It is created slowly over time by the people and by events—by the stories of past success and failure that become a deep part of the company lore. If it's a distinctive culture, it will fit certain people like a custom-made glove. The reason cultures are so stable in time is because people self-select. Someone energized by competitive zeal may select and be happy in one culture, while someone who loves to pioneer and invent may choose another. The world, thankfully, is full of many high-performing, highly distinctive corporate cultures. We never claim that our approach is the right one—just that it's ours—and over the last two decades, we've collected a large group of like-minded people. Folks who find our approach energizing and meaningful.

One area where I think we are especially distinctive is failure. I believe we are the best place in the world to fail (we have plenty of practice!), and failure and invention are inseparable twins. To invent you have to experiment, and if you know in advance that it's going to work, it's not an experiment. Most large organizations embrace the idea of invention but are not willing to suffer the string of failed experiments necessary to get there. Outsized returns often come from betting against conventional wisdom, and conventional wisdom is usually right. Given a ten percent chance of a one hundred times payoff, you should take that bet every time. But you're still going to be wrong nine times out of ten. We all know that if you swing for the fences, you're going to strike out a lot, but you're also going to hit some home runs. The difference between baseball and business, however, is that baseball has a truncated outcome distribution. When you swing, no matter how well you connect with the ball, the most runs you can get is four. In business, every once in a while, when you step up to the plate, you can score one thousand runs. This long-tailed distribution of returns is why it's important to be bold. Big winners pay for so many experiments.

AWS, Marketplace, and Prime are all examples of bold bets at Amazon that worked, and we're fortunate to have those three big pillars. They have helped us grow into a large company, and there are certain things that only large companies can do. With a tip of the hat to our Seattle neighbors, no matter how good an entrepreneur you are, you're not going to build an all-composite 787 in your garage start-up—not one you'd want to fly in anyway. Used well, our scale enables us to build services for customers that we could otherwise never even contemplate. But also, if we're not vigilant and thoughtful, size could slow us down and diminish our inventiveness.

As I meet with teams across Amazon, I am continually amazed at the passion, intelligence, and creativity on display. Our teams accomplished a lot in the last year, and I'd like to share a few of the highlights of our efforts to nourish and globalize our three big offerings—Prime, Marketplace, and AWS. And while I'll focus on those three, I assure you that we also remain hard at work on finding a fourth.

Prime

We want Prime to be such a good value that you'd be irresponsible not to be a member.

We've grown Prime two-day delivery selection from one million items to over thirty million, added Sunday Delivery, and introduced Free Same-Day Delivery on hundreds of thousands of products for customers in more than thirty-five cities around the world. We've added music, photo storage, the Kindle Owners' Lending Library, and streaming films and TV.

Prime Now offers members one-hour delivery on an important subset of selection and was launched only 111 days after it was dreamed up. In that time, a small team built a customer-facing app, secured a location for an urban warehouse, determined which twenty-five thousand items to sell, got those items stocked, recruited and on-boarded new staff, tested, iterated, designed new software for internal use—both a warehouse management system and a driver-facing app—and launched in time for the holidays. Today, just fifteen months after that first city launch, Prime Now is serving members in more than thirty cities around the world.

Prime Video offers exclusives from some of the world's most passionate storytellers. We want brilliant creators like Jill Soloway, Jason Schwartzman, and Spike Lee to take risks and push boundaries. Our original series have already earned more than 120 nominations and won nearly sixty awards, including Golden Globe and Emmy awards. Many of these are stories that might never have been told in the traditional linear programming model. In the pipeline and coming soon are new series and movies from creators like Jeremy Clarkson, David E. Kelley, Woody Allen, and Kenneth Lonergan.

The Man in the High Castle, based on the Philip K. Dick novel, explores an alternate history where the United States lost World War II. It debuted on Prime Video on November 20 and in four weeks became our most-viewed show—receiving acclaim from critics, like "Amazon has the best new drama of the season in *The Man in the High Castle*" and "*The Man in the High Castle* accomplishes so much, where most new broadcast TV dramas these days don't even try."

These shows are great for customers, and they feed the Prime flywheel—Prime members who watch Prime Video are more likely to convert from a free trial to a paid membership, and more likely to renew their annual subscriptions.

Finally, our first ever Prime Day surpassed all our expectations—more new members tried Prime that day than any other day in our history. Worldwide order growth increased 266 percent over the same day the year before, and sellers whose products are Prime-eligible through FBA saw record-breaking sales—with growth nearing 300 percent.

Prime has become an all-you-can-eat, physical-digital hybrid that members love. Membership grew 51 percent last year—including 47 percent growth in the United States and even faster internationally—and there are now tens of millions of members worldwide. There's a good chance you're already one of them, but if you're not—please be responsible—join Prime.

Marketplace

We took two big swings and missed—with Auctions and zShops—before we launched Marketplace over fifteen years ago. We learned from our failures and stayed stubborn on the vision, and today close to 50 percent of units sold on Amazon are sold by third-party sellers. Marketplace is great for customers because it adds unique selection, and it's great for sellers—there are over seventy thousand entrepreneurs with sales of more than $100,000 a year selling on Amazon, and they've created over six hundred thousand new jobs. With FBA, that flywheel spins faster because sellers' inventory becomes Prime-eligible—Prime becomes more valuable for members, and sellers sell more.

This year, we created a new program called Seller Fulfilled Prime. We invited sellers who are able to meet a high bar for shipping speed and consistency in service to be part of the Prime program and ship their own orders at Prime speed directly. Those sellers have already seen a significant bump in sales, and the program has led to hundreds of thousands of additional items that are available to Prime customers via free two-day or next-day shipping in the United States, United Kingdom, and Germany.

We also created the Amazon Lending program to help sellers grow. Since the program launched, we've provided aggregate funding of over $1.5 billion to micro, small and medium businesses across the United States, United Kingdom, and Japan through short-term loans, with a total outstanding loan balance of about $400 million.

Stephen Aarstol, surfer and owner of Tower Paddle Boards, is one beneficiary. His business has become one of the fastest-growing companies in San Diego, in part with a little help from Amazon Lending. Click-to-cash access to capital helps these small enterprises grow, benefits customers with greater selection, and benefits Amazon since our marketplace revenue grows along with the sellers' sales. We hope to expand Amazon Lending and are now working on ways to partner with banks so they can use their expertise to take and manage the bulk of the credit risk.

In addition to nourishing our big offerings, we work to globalize them. Our Marketplace creates opportunities for sellers anywhere to reach buyers around the world. In the past, many sellers would limit their customer base to their home country due to the practical challenges of selling internationally. To globalize Marketplace and expand the opportunities available to sellers, we built selling tools that empowered entrepreneurs in 172 countries to reach customers in 189 countries last year. These cross-border sales are now nearly a quarter of all third-party units sold on Amazon. To make this possible, we translated hundreds of millions of product listings and provided conversion services among forty-four currencies. Even small and niche sellers can now tap into our global customer base and global logistics network. The end result is very different from sellers handling their own one-at-a-time, cross-border fulfillment. Plugable Technologies' CEO, Bernie Thompson, put it this way: "It really changes the paradigm when you're able to ship the goods in bulk to a warehouse in Europe or Japan and have those goods be fulfilled in one day or two days."

India is another example of how we globalize an offering like Marketplace through customer obsession and a passion for invention. Last year we ran a program called Amazon Chai Cart where we deployed three-wheeled mobile carts to navigate in a city's business districts, serve tea, water and lemon juice to small business owners and teach them about selling online. In a period of four months, the team traveled 15,280 kilometers across thirty-one cities, served 37,200 cups of tea and engaged with over ten thousand sellers. Through this program and other conversations with sellers, we found out there was a lot of interest in selling online but that sellers struggled with the belief that the process was time-consuming, tedious, and complex. So, we invented Amazon Tatkal, which enables small businesses to get online in less than sixty minutes. Amazon Tatkal is a specially designed studio-on-wheels offering a suite of launch services including registration, imaging, and cataloguing services, as well as basic seller-training mechanisms. Since its launch on February 17, we have reached sellers in twenty-five cities.

We're also globalizing Fulfillment by Amazon, adapting the service to local customer needs. In India, we launched a program called Seller Flex to combine Amazon's logistics capabilities with sellers' selection at the local neighborhood level. Sellers set aside a part of their warehouse for storing items to be sold on Amazon, and we configure it as a fulfillment center in our network that can receive and fulfill customer orders. Our team provides guidance on warehouse layout, IT and operational infrastructure, and trains the seller on standard operating procedures to be followed onsite. We've now launched twenty-five operational Seller Flex sites across ten cities.

Amazon Web Services

Just over ten years ago, AWS started in the United States with its first major service, a simple storage service. Today, AWS offers more than seventy services for compute, storage, databases, analytics, mobile, Internet of Things, and enterprise applications. We also offer thirty-three availability zones across twelve geographic regions worldwide, with another five regions and eleven availability zones in Canada, China, India, the United States, and the United Kingdom to be available in the coming year. AWS started with developers and start-ups, and now is used by more than a million customers from organizations of every size across nearly every industry—companies like Pinterest, Airbnb, GE, Enel, Capital One, Intuit, Johnson & Johnson, Philips, Hess, Adobe, McDonald's, and Time Inc.

AWS is bigger than Amazon.com was at ten years old, growing at a faster rate, and—most noteworthy in my view—the pace of innovation continues to accelerate—we announced 722 significant new features and services in 2015, a 40 percent increase over 2014.

Many characterized AWS as a bold—and unusual—bet when we started. "What does this have to do with selling books?" We could have stuck to the knitting. I'm glad we didn't. Or did we? Maybe the knitting has as much to do with our approach as the arena. AWS is customer obsessed, inventive and experimental, long-term oriented, and cares deeply about operational excellence.

Given ten years and many iterations, that approach has allowed AWS to rapidly expand into the world's most comprehensive, widely adopted cloud service. As with our retail business, AWS is made up of many small teams with single-threaded owners, enabling rapid innovation. The team rolls out new functionality almost daily across seventy services, and that new functionality just "shows up" for customers—there's no upgrading.

Many companies describe themselves as customer-focused, but few walk the walk. Most big technology companies are competitor focused. They see what others are doing, and then work to fast follow. In contrast, 90 to 95 percent of what we build in AWS is driven by what customers tell us they want. A good example is our new database engine, Amazon Aurora. Customers have been frustrated by the proprietary nature, high cost, and licensing terms of traditional, commercial-grade database providers. And while many companies have started moving toward more open engines like MySQL and Postgres, they often struggle to get the performance they need. Customers asked us if we could eliminate that inconvenient trade-off, and that's why we built Aurora. It has commercial-grade durability and availability, is fully compatible with MySQL, has up to five times better performance than the typical MySQL implementation, but is one-tenth the price of the traditional, commercial-grade database engines. This has struck a resonant chord with customers, and Aurora is the fastest-growing service in the history of AWS. Nearly this same story could be told about Redshift, our managed data warehouse service, which is the second fastest growing service in AWS history—both small and large companies are moving their data warehouses to Redshift.

Our approach to pricing is also driven by our customer-centric culture—we've dropped prices fifty-one times, in many cases before there was any competitive pressure to do so. In addition to price reductions, we've also continued to launch new lower cost services like Aurora, Redshift, QuickSight (our new Business Intelligence service), EC2 Container Service (our new compute container service), and Lambda (our pioneering server-less computing capability), while extending our services to offer a range of highly cost-effective options for running just about every type of application or IT use case imaginable. We even roll out and continuously improve services like Trusted Advisor, which alerts customers when they can save money—resulting in hundreds of millions of dollars in savings for our customers. I'm pretty sure we're the only IT vendor telling customers how to stop spending money with us.

Whether you are a start-up founded yesterday or a business that has been around for 140 years, the cloud is providing all of us with unbelievable opportunities to reinvent our businesses, add new customer experiences, redeploy capital to fuel growth, increase security, and do all of this so much faster than before. MLB Advanced Media is an example of an AWS customer that is constantly reinventing the customer experience. MLB's Statcast tracking technology is a new feature for baseball fans that measures the position of each player, the baserunners, and the ball as they move during every play on the field, giving viewers on any screen access to empirical data that answers age-old questions like "What could have happened if . . ." while also bringing new questions to life. Turning baseball into rocket science, Statcast uses a missile radar system to measure every pitched ball's movements more than two thousand times per second, streams and collects data in real-time through Amazon Kinesis (our service for processing real-time streaming data), stores the data on Amazon S3, and then performs analytics in Amazon EC2. The suite of services will generate nearly 7 TB of raw statistical data per game and up to 17 PB per season, shedding quantitative light on age-old, but never verified, baseball pearls of wisdom like "never slide into first."

About seven years ago, Netflix announced that they were going to move all their applications to the cloud. Netflix chose AWS because it provided them with the greatest scale and the broadest set of services and features. Netflix recently completed their cloud migration, and stories like theirs are becoming increasingly common as companies like Infor, Intuit, and Time Inc. have made plans to move all of their applications to AWS.

AWS is already good enough today to attract more than one million customers, and the service is only going to get better from here. As the team continues their rapid pace of innovation, we'll offer more and more capabilities to let builders build unfettered, it will get easier and easier to collect, store and analyze data, we'll continue to add more geographic locations, and we'll continue to see growth in mobile and "connected" device applications. Over time, it's likely that most companies will choose not to run their own data centers, opting for the cloud instead.

Invention Machine

We want to be a large company that's also an invention machine. We want to combine the extraordinary customer-serving capabilities that are enabled by size with the speed of movement, nimbleness, and risk-acceptance mentality normally associated with entrepreneurial start-ups.

Can we do it? I'm optimistic. We have a good start on it, and I think our culture puts us in a position to achieve the goal. But I don't think it'll be easy. There are some subtle traps that even high-performing large organizations can fall into as a matter of course, and we'll have to learn as an institution how to guard against them. One common pitfall for large organizations—one that hurts speed and inventiveness—is "one-size-fits-all" decision making.

Some decisions are consequential and irreversible or nearly irreversible—one-way doors—and these decisions must be made methodically, carefully, slowly, with great deliberation and consultation. If you walk through and don't like what you see on the other side, you can't get back to where you were before. We can call these Type 1 decisions. But most decisions aren't like that—they are changeable, reversible—they're two-way doors. If you've made a suboptimal Type 2 decision, you don't have to live with the consequences for that long. You can reopen the door and go back through. Type 2 decisions can and should be made quickly by high judgment individuals or small groups.

As organizations get larger, there seems to be a tendency to use the heavy-weight Type 1 decision-making *process* on most decisions, including many Type 2 decisions. The end result of this is slowness, unthoughtful risk aversion, failure to experiment sufficiently, and consequently diminished invention.* We'll have to figure out how to fight that tendency.

And one-size-fits-all thinking will turn out to be only one of the pitfalls. We'll work hard to avoid it—and any other large organization maladies we can identify.

Sustainability and Social Invention

Our growth has happened fast. Twenty years ago, I was driving boxes to the post office in my Chevy Blazer and dreaming of a forklift. In absolute numbers (as opposed to percentages), the past few years

---

*The opposite situation is less interesting and there is undoubtedly some survivorship bias. Any companies that habitually use the light-weight Type 2 decision-making process to make Type 1 decisions go extinct before they get large.

have been especially significant. We've grown from 30,000 employees in 2010 to more than 230,000 now. We're a bit like parents who look around one day and realize their kids are grown—you blink, and it happens.

One thing that's exciting about our current scale is that we can put our inventive culture to work on moving the needle on sustainability and social issues.

Two years ago we set a long-term goal to use 100 percent renewable energy across our global AWS infrastructure. We've since announced four significant wind and solar farms that will deliver 1.6 million megawatt hours per year of additional renewable energy into the electric grids that supply AWS data centers. Amazon Wind Farm Fowler Ridge has already come online. We reached 25 percent sustainable energy use across AWS last year, are on track to reach 40 percent this year, and are working on goals that will cover all of Amazon's facilities around the world, including our fulfillment centers.

We'll keep expanding our efforts in areas like packaging, where our culture of invention led to a big winner—the Frustration-Free Packaging program. Seven years ago we introduced the initiative with nineteen products. Today, there are more than four hundred thousand globally. In 2015, the program eliminated tens of millions of pounds of excess packaging material. Frustration-Free Packaging is a customer delighter because the packages are easier to open. It's good for the planet because it creates less waste. And it's good for shareholders because, with tighter packaging, we ship less "air" and save on transportation costs.

We also continue to pioneer new programs for employees—like Career Choice, Leave Share, and Ramp Back. Career Choice prepays 95 percent of tuition for courses that teach in-demand skills, regardless of whether those skills are relevant to a career at Amazon. We'll pay for nursing certifications, airplane mechanic courses, and many others. We're building classrooms with glass walls right in our fulfillment centers as a way to encourage employees to participate in the program and to make it easy. We see the impact through stories like Sharie Warmack—a single mother of eight who worked in one of our Phoenix fulfillment centers. Career Choice paid for Sharie to get licensed to drive an eighteen-wheeler. Sharie worked hard, passed her tests, and she's now a long-haul driver for Schneider Trucking—and loving it. This coming year, we're launching a program to teach other interested companies the benefits of Career Choice and how to implement it.

Leave Share and Ramp Back are programs that give new parents flexibility with their growing families. Leave Share lets employees share their Amazon paid leave with their spouse or domestic partner if their spouse's employer doesn't offer paid leave. Ramp Back gives birth mothers additional control over the pace at which they return to work. Just as with our health care plan, these benefits are egalitarian—they're the same for our fulfillment center and customer service employees as they are for our most senior executives.

Renewable energy, Frustration-Free Packaging, Career Choice, Leave Share, and Ramp Back are examples of a culture that embraces invention and long-term thinking. It's very energizing to think that our scale provides opportunities to create impact in these areas.

I can tell you it's a great joy for me to get to work every day with a team of such smart, imaginative, and passionate people.

It's still Day 1.

Fending Off Day 2

2016

"**J**EFF, WHAT DOES Day 2 look like?"

That's a question I just got at our most recent all-hands meeting. I've been reminding people that it's Day 1 for a couple of decades. I work in an Amazon building named Day 1, and when I moved buildings, I took the name with me. I spend time thinking about this topic.

"Day 2 is stasis. Followed by irrelevance. Followed by excruciating, painful decline. Followed by death. And *that* is why it is *always* Day 1."

To be sure, this kind of decline would happen in extreme slow motion. An established company might harvest Day 2 for decades, but the final result would still come.

I'm interested in the question "How do you fend off Day 2?" What are the techniques and tactics? How do you keep the vitality of Day 1, even inside a large organization?

Such a question can't have a simple answer. There will be many elements, multiple paths, and many traps. I don't know the whole answer, but I may know bits of it. Here's a starter pack of essentials for Day 1 defense: customer obsession, a skeptical view of proxies, the eager adoption of external trends, and high-velocity decision making.

True Customer Obsession

There are many ways to center a business. You can be competitor focused, you can be product focused, you can be technology focused, you can be business model focused, and there are more. But in my view, obsessive customer focus is by far the most protective of Day 1 vitality.

Why? There are many advantages to a customer-centric approach, but here's the big one: customers are *always* beautifully, wonderfully dissatisfied, even when they report being happy and business is great. Even when they don't yet know it, customers want something better, and your desire to delight customers will drive you to invent on their behalf. No customer ever asked Amazon to create the Prime membership program, but it sure turns out they wanted it, and I could give you many such examples.

Staying in Day 1 requires you to experiment patiently, accept failures, plant seeds, protect saplings, and double down when you see customer delight. A customer-obsessed culture best creates the conditions where all of that can happen.

Resist Proxies

As companies get larger and more complex, there's a tendency to manage to proxies. This comes in many shapes and sizes, and it's dangerous, subtle, and very Day 2.

A common example is process as proxy. Good process serves you so you can serve customers. But if you're not watchful, the process can become the thing. This can happen very easily in large organizations. The process becomes the proxy for the result you want. You stop looking at outcomes and just make sure you're doing the process right. Gulp. It's not that rare to hear a junior leader defend a bad outcome with something like, "Well, we followed the process." A more experienced leader will use it as an opportunity to investigate and improve the process. The process is not the thing. It's always worth asking, do we own the process or does the process own us? In a Day 2 company, you might find it's the second.

Another example: market research and customer surveys can become proxies for customers—something that's especially dangerous when you're inventing and designing products. "Fifty-five percent of beta testers report being satisfied with this feature. That is up from 47 percent in the first survey." That's hard to interpret and could unintentionally mislead.

Good inventors and designers *deeply* understand their customer. They spend tremendous energy developing that intuition. They study and understand many anecdotes rather than only the averages you'll find on surveys. They *live* with the design.

I'm not against beta testing or surveys. But you, the product or service owner, must understand the customer, have a vision, and love the offering. Then, beta testing and research can help you find your blind spots. A remarkable customer experience starts with heart, intuition, curiosity, play, guts, taste. You won't find any of it in a survey.

Embrace External Trends

The outside world can push you into Day 2 if you won't or can't embrace powerful trends quickly. If you fight them, you're probably fighting the future. Embrace them and you have a tailwind.

These big trends are not that hard to spot (they get talked and written about a lot), but they can be strangely hard for large organizations to embrace. We're in the middle of an obvious one right now: machine learning and artificial intelligence.

Over the past decades, computers have broadly automated tasks that programmers could describe with clear rules and algorithms. Modern machine learning techniques now allow us to do the same for tasks where describing the precise rules is much harder.

At Amazon, we've been engaged in the practical application of machine learning for many years now. Some of this work is highly visible: our autonomous Prime Air delivery drones; the Amazon Go convenience store that uses machine vision to eliminate checkout lines; and Alexa,* our cloud-based AI assistant. (We still struggle to keep Echo in stock, despite our best efforts. A high-quality problem, but a problem. We're working on it.)

But much of what we do with machine learning happens beneath the surface. Machine learning drives our algorithms for demand forecasting, product search ranking, product and deals recommendations, merchandising placements, fraud detection, translations, and much more. Though less visible, much of the impact of machine learning will be of this type—quietly but meaningfully improving core operations.

Inside AWS, we're excited to lower the costs and barriers to machine learning and AI so organizations of all sizes can take advantage of these advanced techniques.

Using our prepackaged versions of popular deep learning frameworks running on P2 compute instances (optimized for this workload), customers are already developing powerful systems ranging everywhere from early disease detection to increasing crop yields. And we've also made Amazon's higher-level services available in a convenient form. Amazon Lex (what's inside Alexa), Amazon Polly, and Amazon Rekognition remove the heavy lifting from natural language understanding, speech generation, and image analysis. They

---

*For something amusing, try asking, "Alexa, what is sixty factorial?"

can be accessed with simple API calls—no machine learning expertise required. Watch this space. Much more to come.

High-Velocity Decision Making

Day 2 companies make high-*quality* decisions, but they make
high-quality decisions *slowly*. To keep the energy and dynamism
of Day 1, you have to somehow make high-quality, *high-velocity*
decisions. Easy for start-ups and very challenging for large organizations. The senior team at Amazon is determined to keep our
decision-making velocity high. Speed matters in business—plus a
high-velocity decision-making environment is more fun too. We
don't know all the answers, but here are some thoughts.

First, never use a one-size-fits-all decision-making process. Many
decisions are reversible, two-way doors. Those decisions can use
a light-weight process. For those, so what if you're wrong? I wrote
about this in more detail in last year's letter.

Second, most decisions should probably be made with somewhere around 70 percent of the information you wish you had. If
you wait for 90 percent, in most cases, you're probably being slow.
Plus, either way, you need to be good at quickly recognizing and
correcting bad decisions. If you're good at course correcting, being
wrong may be less costly than you think, whereas being slow is going
to be expensive for sure.

Third, use the phrase "disagree and commit." This phrase will
save a lot of time. If you have conviction on a particular direction
even though there's no consensus, it's helpful to say, "Look, I know
we disagree on this, but will you gamble with me on it? Disagree
and commit?" By the time you're at this point, no one can know the
answer for sure, and you'll probably get a quick yes.

This isn't one way. If you're the boss, you should do this too. I disagree and commit all the time. We recently greenlit a particular Amazon Studios original. I told the team my view: debatable whether

it would be interesting enough, complicated to produce, the business terms aren't that good, and we have lots of other opportunities. They had a completely different opinion and wanted to go ahead. I wrote back right away with "I disagree and commit and hope it becomes the most watched thing we've ever made." Consider how much slower this decision cycle would have been if the team had actually had to *convince* me rather than simply get my commitment.

Note what this example is not: it's not me thinking to myself "Well, these guys are wrong and missing the point, but this isn't worth me chasing." It's a genuine disagreement of opinion, a candid expression of my view, a chance for the team to weigh my view, and a quick, sincere commitment to go their way. And given that this team has already brought home eleven Emmys, six Golden Globes, and three Oscars, I'm just glad they let me in the room at all!

Fourth, recognize true *misalignment* issues early and escalate them *immediately*. Sometimes teams have different objectives and fundamentally different views. They are not aligned. No amount of discussion, no number of meetings will resolve that deep misalignment. Without escalation, the default dispute resolution mechanism for this scenario is exhaustion. Whoever has more stamina carries the decision.

I've seen many examples of sincere misalignment at Amazon over the years. When we decided to invite third-party sellers to compete directly against us on our own product detail pages—that was a big one. Many smart, well-intentioned Amazonians were simply not at all aligned with the direction. The big decision set up hundreds of smaller decisions, many of which needed to be escalated to the senior team.

"You've worn me down" is an awful decision-making process. It's slow and de-energizing. Go for quick escalation instead—it's better.

So, have you settled only for decision quality, or are you mindful of decision velocity too? Are the world's trends tailwinds for you? Are you falling prey to proxies, or do they serve you? And most important of all, are you delighting customers? We can have the scope

Building a Culture of
High Standards

2017

THE AMERICAN CUSTOMER Satisfaction Index recently announced the results of its annual survey, and for the eighth year in a row, customers ranked Amazon #1. The United Kingdom has a similar index, the UK Customer Satisfaction Index, put out by the Institute of Customer Service. For the fifth time in a row Amazon UK ranked #1 in that survey. Amazon was also just named the #1 business on LinkedIn's 2018 Top Companies list, which ranks the most sought-after places to work for professionals in the United States. And just a few weeks ago, Harris Poll released its annual Reputation Quotient, which surveys over twenty-five thousand consumers on a broad range of topics from workplace environment to social responsibility to products and services, and for the third year in a row Amazon ranked #1.

Congratulations and thank you to the now over 560,000 Amazonians who come to work every day with unrelenting customer obsession, ingenuity, and commitment to operational excellence. And on behalf of Amazonians everywhere, I want to extend a huge thank-you to customers. It's incredibly energizing for us to see your responses to these surveys.

One thing I love about customers is that they are divinely discontent. Their expectations are never static—they go up. It's human nature. We didn't ascend from our hunter-gatherer days by being satisfied. People have a voracious appetite for a better way, and yesterday's "wow" quickly becomes today's "ordinary." I see that cycle of improvement happening at a faster rate than ever before. It may be because customers have such easy access to more information than ever before—in only a few seconds and with a couple taps on their phones, customers can read reviews, compare prices from multiple retailers, see whether something's in stock, find out how fast it will ship or be available for pickup, and more. These examples are from retail, but I sense that the same customer empowerment phenomenon is happening broadly across everything we do at Amazon and most other industries as well. You cannot rest on your laurels in this world. Customers won't have it.

How do you stay ahead of ever-rising customer expectations? There's no single way to do it—it's a combination of many things. But high standards (widely deployed and at all levels of detail) are certainly a big part of it. We've had some successes over the years in our quest to meet the high expectations of customers. We've also had billions of dollars' worth of failures along the way. With those experiences as backdrop, I'd like to share with you the essentials of what we've learned (so far) about high standards inside an organization.

Intrinsic or Teachable?

First, there's a foundational question: are high standards intrinsic or teachable? If you take me on your basketball team, you can teach me many things, but you can't teach me to be taller. Do we first and foremost need to select for "high standards" people? If so, this letter would need to be mostly about hiring practices, but I don't think so. I believe high standards are teachable. In fact, people are pretty good at learning high standards simply through exposure. High standards are contagious. Bring a new person onto a high standards team, and they'll quickly adapt. The opposite is also true. If low standards prevail, those too will quickly spread. And though exposure works well to teach high standards, I believe you can accelerate that rate of learning by articulating a few core principles of high standards, which I hope to share in this letter.

Universal or Domain Specific?

Another important question is whether high standards are universal or domain specific. In other words, if you have high standards in one area, do you automatically have high standards elsewhere? I believe high standards are domain specific, and that you have to learn high standards separately in every arena of interest. When I started Amazon, I had high standards on inventing, on customer care, and (thankfully) on hiring. But I didn't have high standards on operational process: how to keep fixed problems fixed, how to eliminate defects at the root, how to inspect processes, and much more. I had to learn and develop high standards on all of that (my colleagues were my tutors).

Understanding this point is important because it keeps you humble. You can consider yourself a person of high standards in general and still have debilitating blind spots. There can be whole arenas of endeavor where you may not even know that your standards are low or nonexistent, and certainly not world class. It's critical to be open to that likelihood.

Recognition and Scope

What do you need to achieve high standards in a particular domain area? First, you have to be able to recognize what good looks like in that domain. Second, you must have realistic expectations for how hard it should be (how much work it will take) to achieve that result—the scope.

Let me give you two examples. One is a sort of toy illustration, but it makes the point clearly, and another is a real one that comes up at Amazon all the time.

Perfect Handstands

A close friend recently decided to learn to do a perfect free-standing handstand. No leaning against a wall. Not for just a few seconds. Instagram good. She decided to start her journey by taking a handstand workshop at her yoga studio. She then practiced for a while but wasn't getting the results she wanted. So, she hired a handstand coach. Yes, I know what you're thinking, but evidently this is an actual thing that exists. In the very first lesson, the coach gave her some wonderful advice. "Most people," he said, "think that if they work hard, they should be able to master a handstand in about two weeks. The reality is that it takes about six months of daily practice. If you think you should be able to do it in two weeks, you're just going to end up quitting." Unrealistic beliefs on scope—often hidden and undiscussed—kill high standards. To achieve high standards yourself or as part of a team, you need to form and proactively communicate realistic beliefs about how hard something is going to be—something this coach understood well.

Six-Page Narratives

We don't do PowerPoint (or any other slide-oriented) presentations at Amazon. Instead, we write narratively structured six-page memos. We silently read one at the beginning of each meeting in a kind of "study hall." Not surprisingly, the quality of these memos varies widely. Some have the clarity of angels singing. They are brilliant and thoughtful and set up the meeting for high-quality discussion. Sometimes they come in at the other end of the spectrum.

In the handstand example, it's pretty straightforward to recognize high standards. It wouldn't be difficult to lay out in detail the requirements of a well-executed handstand, and then you're either doing it or you're not. The writing example is very different. The difference between a great memo and an average one is much squishier. It would be extremely hard to write down the detailed requirements that make up a great memo. Nevertheless, I find that much of the time, readers react to great memos very similarly. They know it when they see it. The standard is there, and it is real, even if it's not easily describable.

Here's what we've figured out. Often, when a memo isn't great, it's not the writer's inability to recognize the high standard, but instead a wrong expectation on scope: they mistakenly believe a high-standards, six-page memo can be written in one or two days or even a few hours, when really it might take a week or more! They're trying to perfect a handstand in just two weeks, and we're not coaching them right. The great memos are written and re-written, shared with colleagues who are asked to improve the work, set aside for a couple of days, and then edited again with a fresh mind. They simply can't be done in a day or two. The key point here is that you can improve results through the simple act of teaching scope—that a great memo probably should take a week or more.

Skill

Beyond recognizing the standard and having realistic expectations on scope, how about skill? Surely to write a world-class memo, you have to be an extremely skilled writer. Is it another required element? In my view, not so much, at least not for the individual in the context of teams. The football coach doesn't need to be able to throw, and a film director doesn't need to be able to act. But they both do need to recognize high standards for those things and teach realistic expectations on scope. Even in the example of writing a six-page memo, that's teamwork. Someone on the team needs to have the skill, but it doesn't have to be you. (As a side note, by tradition at Amazon, authors' names never appear on the memos—the memo is from the whole team.)

Benefits of High Standards

Building a culture of high standards is well worth the effort, and there are many benefits. Naturally and most obviously, you're going to build better products and services for customers—this would be reason enough! Perhaps a little less obvious: people are drawn to high standards—they help with recruiting and retention. More subtle: a culture of high standards is protective of all the "invisible" but crucial work that goes on in every company. I'm talking about the work that no one sees. The work that gets done when no one is watching. In a high standards culture, doing that work well is its own reward—it's part of what it means to be a professional.

And finally, high standards are fun! Once you've tasted high standards, there's no going back.

So, the four elements of high standards as we see it: they are teachable, they are domain specific, you must recognize them, and you must explicitly coach realistic scope. For us, these work at all levels of detail. Everything from writing memos to whole new, clean-sheet business initiatives. We hope they help you too.

Insist on the Highest Standards

Leaders have relentlessly high standards—many people may think these standards are unreasonably high.

—from the Amazon Leadership Principles

Recent Milestones

The high standards our leaders strive for have served us well. And while I certainly can't do a handstand myself, I'm extremely proud to share some of the milestones we hit last year, each of which represents the fruition of many years of collective effort. We take none of them for granted.

Prime: Thirteen years post-launch, we have exceeded one hundred million paid Prime members globally. In 2017 Amazon shipped more than five billion items with Prime worldwide, and more new members joined Prime than in any previous year—both worldwide and in the United States. Members in the United States now receive unlimited free two-day shipping on over one hundred million different items. We expanded Prime to Mexico, Singapore, the Netherlands, and Luxembourg, and introduced Business Prime Shipping in the United States and Germany. We keep making Prime shipping faster as well, with Prime Free Same-Day and Prime Free One-Day delivery now in more than eight thousand cities and towns. Prime Now is available in more than fifty cities worldwide across nine countries. Prime Day 2017 was our biggest global shopping event ever (until surpassed by Cyber Monday), with more new Prime members joining Prime than any other day in our history.

AWS: It's exciting to see Amazon Web Services, a $20 billion revenue run rate business, accelerate its already healthy growth. AWS has also accelerated its pace of innovation—especially in new areas such as machine learning and artificial intelligence, Internet of Things, and serverless computing. In 2017, AWS announced more than fourteen hundred significant services and features, including Amazon SageMaker, which radically changes the accessibility and ease of use for everyday developers to build sophisticated machine learning models. Tens of thousands of customers are also using a broad range of AWS machine learning services, with active users increasing more than 250 percent in the last year, spurred by the broad adoption of Amazon SageMaker. And in November, we held our sixth re:Invent conference with more than forty thousand attendees and over sixty thousand streaming participants.

Marketplace: In 2017, for the first time in our history, more than half of the units sold on Amazon worldwide were from our third-party sellers, including small and medium-sized businesses (SMBs). Over three hundred thousand US-based SMBs started selling on Amazon in 2017, and Fulfillment by Amazon shipped billions of items for SMBs worldwide. Customers ordered more than forty million items from SMBs worldwide during Prime Day 2017, growing their sales by more than 60 percent over Prime Day 2016. Our Global Selling program (enabling SMBs to sell products across national borders) grew by over 50 percent in 2017 and cross-border ecommerce by SMBs now represents more than 25 percent of total third-party sales.

Alexa: Customer embrace of Alexa continues, with Alexa-enabled devices among the best-selling items across all of Amazon. We're seeing extremely strong adoption by other companies and developers that want to create their own experiences with Alexa. There are now more than thirty thousand skills for Alexa from outside developers, and customers can control more than four thousand smart home devices from twelve hundred unique brands with Alexa. The foundations of Alexa continue to get smarter every day too. We've developed and implemented an on-device fingerprinting technique, which keeps your device from waking up when it hears an Alexa commercial on TV. (This technology ensured that our Alexa Super Bowl commercial didn't wake up millions of devices.) Far-field speech recognition (already very good) has improved by 15 percent over the last year; and in the United States, United Kingdom, and Germany, we've improved Alexa's spoken language understanding by more than 25 percent over the last twelve months through enhancements in Alexa's machine learning components and the use of semi-supervised learning techniques. (These semi-supervised learning techniques reduced the amount of labeled data needed to achieve the same accuracy improvement by forty times!) Finally, we've dramatically reduced the amount of time required to teach Alexa new languages by using machine translation and transfer learning techniques, which allows us to serve customers in more countries (like India and Japan).

Amazon devices: 2017 was our best year yet for hardware sales. Customers bought tens of millions of Echo devices, and Echo Dot and Fire TV Stick with Alexa were the best-selling products across all of Amazon—across all categories and all manufacturers. Customers bought twice as many Fire TV Sticks and Kids Edition Fire Tablets this holiday season versus last year. 2017 marked the release of our all-new Echo with an improved design, better sound, and a lower price; Echo Plus with a built-in smart home hub; and Echo Spot, which is compact and beautiful with a circular screen. We released our next generation Fire TV, featuring 4K Ultra HD and HDR; and the Fire HD 10 Tablet, with 1080p Full HD display. And we celebrated the tenth anniversary of Kindle by releasing the all-new Kindle Oasis, our most advanced reader ever. It's waterproof—take it in the bathtub—with a bigger 7-inch, high-resolution, 300 ppi display and has built-in audio so you can also listen to your books with Audible.

Prime Video: Prime Video continues to drive Prime member adoption and retention. In the last year we made Prime Video even better for customers by adding new, award-winning Prime Originals to the service, like *The Marvelous Mrs. Maisel,* winner of two Critics' Choice Awards and two Golden Globes, and the Oscar-nominated movie *The Big Sick.* We've expanded our slate of programming across the globe, launching new seasons of *Bosch* and *Sneaky Pete* from the United States, *The Grand Tour* from the United Kingdom, and *You Are Wanted* from Germany, while adding new *Sentosha* shows from Japan, along with *Breathe* and the award-winning *Inside Edge* from India. Also this year, we expanded our Prime Channels offerings, adding CBS All Access in the United States and launching channels in the United Kingdom and Germany. We debuted NFL Thursday Night Football on Prime Video, with more than eighteen million total viewers over eleven games. In 2017, Prime Video Direct secured subscription video rights for more than three thousand feature films and committed over $18 million in royalties to independent filmmakers and other rights holders. Looking forward, we're also excited about our upcoming Prime Original series pipeline, which includes Tom Clancy's *Jack Ryan* starring John Krasinski; *King Lear*, starring Anthony Hopkins and Emma Thompson; *The Romanoffs*, executive-produced by Matt Weiner; *Carnival Row* starring Orlando Bloom and Cara Delevingne; *Good Omens* starring Jon Hamm; and *Homecoming*, executive-produced by Sam Esmail and starring Julia Roberts in her first television series. We acquired the global television rights for a multiseason production of *The Lord of the Rings*, as well as *Cortés*, a miniseries based on the epic saga of Hernán Cortés from executive producer Steven Spielberg, starring Javier Bardem, and we look forward to beginning work on those shows this year.

Amazon Music: Amazon Music continues to grow fast and now has tens of millions of paid customers. Amazon Music Unlimited, our on-demand, ad-free offering, expanded to more than thirty new countries in 2017, and membership has more than doubled over the past six months.

Fashion: Amazon has become the destination for tens of millions of customers to shop for fashion. In 2017, we introduced our first fashion-oriented Prime benefit, Prime Wardrobe—a new service that brings the fitting room directly to the homes of Prime members so they can try on the latest styles before they buy. We introduced Nike and UGG on Amazon along with new celebrity collections by Drew Barrymore and Dwyane Wade, as well as dozens of new private brands, like Goodthreads and Core10. We're also continuing to enable thousands of designers and artists to offer their exclusive designs and prints on demand through Merch by Amazon. We finished 2017 with the launch of our interactive shopping experience with Calvin Klein, including pop-up shops, on-site product customization, and fitting rooms with Alexa-controlled lighting, music, and more.

Whole Foods: When we closed our acquisition of Whole Foods Market last year, we announced our commitment to making high-quality, natural and organic food available for everyone, then immediately lowered prices on a selection of best-selling grocery staples, including avocados, organic brown eggs, and responsibly farmed salmon. We followed this with a second round of price reductions in November, and our Prime member exclusive promotion broke Whole Foods' all-time record for turkeys sold during the Thanksgiving season. In February, we introduced free two-hour delivery on orders over $35 for Prime members in select cities, followed by additional cities in March and April, and plan continued expansion across the United States throughout this year. We also expanded the benefits of the Amazon Prime Rewards Visa Card, enabling Prime members to get 5 percent back when shopping at Whole Foods Market. Beyond that, customers can purchase Whole Foods' private label products like 365 Everyday Value on Amazon, purchase Echo and other Amazon devices in over a hundred Whole Foods stores, and pick up or return Amazon packages at Amazon Lockers in hundreds of Whole Foods stores. We've also begun the technical work needed to recognize Prime members at the point of sale and look forward to offering more Prime benefits to Whole Foods shoppers once that work is completed.

Amazon Go: Amazon Go, a new kind of store with no checkout required, opened to the public in January in Seattle. Since opening, we've been thrilled to hear many customers refer to their shopping experience as "magical." What makes the magic possible is a custom-built combination of computer vision, sensor fusion, and deep learning, which come together to create Just Walk Out shopping. With JWO, customers are able to grab their favorite breakfast, lunch, dinner, snack, and grocery essentials more conveniently than ever before. Some of our top-selling items are not surprising—caffeinated beverages and water are popular—but our customers also love the Chicken Banh Mi sandwich, chocolate chip cookies, cut fruit, gummy bears, and our Amazon Meal Kits.

Treasure Truck: Treasure Truck expanded from a single truck in Seattle to a fleet of thirty-five trucks across twenty-five US cities and twelve UK cities. Our bubble-blowing, music-pumping trucks fulfilled hundreds of thousands of orders, from porterhouse steaks to the latest Nintendo releases. Throughout the year, Treasure Truck also partnered with local communities to lift spirits and help those in need, including donating and delivering hundreds of car seats, thousands of toys, tens of thousands of socks, and many other essentials to community members needing relief, from those displaced by Hurricane Harvey, to the homeless, to kids needing holiday cheer.

India: Amazon.in is the fastest growing marketplace in India, and the most visited site on both desktop and mobile, according to comScore and SimilarWeb. The Amazon.in mobile shopping app was also the most downloaded shopping app in India in 2017, according to App Annie. Prime added more members in India in its first year than any previous geography in Amazon's history. Prime selection in India now includes more than forty million local products from third-party sellers, and Prime Video is investing in Indian original video content in a big way, including two recent premiers and over a dozen new shows in production.

Sustainability: We are committed to minimizing carbon emissions by optimizing our transportation network, improving product packaging, and enhancing energy efficiency in our operations, and we have a long-term goal to power our global infrastructure using 100 percent renewable energy. We recently launched Amazon Wind Farm Texas, our largest wind farm yet, which generates more than one million megawatt hours of clean energy annually from over one hundred turbines. We have plans to host solar energy systems at fifty fulfillment centers by 2020 and have launched twenty-four wind and solar projects across the United States with more than twenty-nine additional projects to come. Together, Amazon's renewable energy projects now produce enough clean energy to power over 330,000 homes annually. In 2017 we celebrated the ten-year anniversary of Frustration-Free Packaging, the first of a suite of sustainable packaging initiatives that have eliminated more than 244,000 tons of packaging materials over the past ten years. In addition, in 2017 alone our programs significantly reduced packaging waste, eliminating the equivalent of 305 million shipping boxes. And across the world, Amazon is contracting with our service providers to launch our first low-pollution last-mile fleet. Already today, a portion of our European delivery fleet is comprised of low-pollution electric and natural gas vans and cars, and we have over forty electric scooters and e-cargo bikes that complete local urban deliveries.

Empowering small business: Millions of small and medium-sized businesses worldwide now sell their products through Amazon to reach new customers around the globe. SMBs selling on Amazon come from every state in the United States, and from more than 130 different countries around the world. More than 140,000 SMBs surpassed $100,000 in sales on Amazon in 2017, and over a thousand independent authors surpassed $100,000 in royalties in 2017 through Kindle Direct Publishing.

Investment and job creation: Since 2011, we have invested over $150 billion worldwide in our fulfillment networks, transportation capabilities, and technology infrastructure, including AWS data centers. Amazon has created over 1.7 million direct and indirect jobs around the world. In 2017 alone, we directly created more than 130,000 new Amazon jobs, not including acquisitions, bringing our global employee base to over 560,000. Our new jobs cover a wide range of professions, from artificial intelligence scientists to packaging specialists to fulfillment center associates. In addition to these direct hires, we estimate that Amazon Marketplace has created 900,000 more jobs worldwide, and that Amazon's investments have created an additional 260,000 jobs in areas like construction, logistics, and other professional services.

Career Choice: One employee program we're particularly proud of is Amazon Career Choice. For hourly associates with more than one year of tenure, we prepay 95 percent of tuition, fees, and textbooks (up to $12,000) for certificates and associate degrees in high-demand occupations such as aircraft mechanics, computer-aided design, machine tool technologies, medical lab technologies, and nursing. We fund education in areas that are in high demand and do so regardless of whether those skills are relevant to a career at Amazon. Globally more than sixteen thousand associates (including more than twelve thousand in the United States) have joined Career Choice since the program launched in 2012. Career Choice is live in ten countries and expanding to South Africa, Costa Rica, and Slovakia later this year. Commercial truck driving, health care, and information technology are the program's most popular fields of study. We've built thirty-nine Career Choice classrooms so far, and we locate them behind glass walls in high traffic areas inside our fulfillment centers so associates can be inspired by seeing their peers pursue new skills.

The credit for these milestones is deserved by many. Amazon is 560,000 employees. It's also two million sellers, hundreds of thousands of authors, millions of AWS developers, and hundreds of millions of divinely discontent customers around the world who push to make us better each and every day.

Path Ahead

This year marks the twentieth anniversary of our first shareholder letter, and our core values and approach remain unchanged. We continue to aspire to be Earth's most customer-centric company, and we recognize this to be no small or easy challenge. We know there is much we can do better, and we find tremendous energy in the many challenges and opportunities that lie ahead.

A huge thank-you to each and every customer for allowing us to serve you, to our shareowners for your support, and to Amazonians everywhere for your ingenuity, your passion, and your high standards.

It remains Day 1.

Intuition, Curiosity, and the Power of Wandering

2018

SOMETHING STRANGE AND remarkable has happened over the last twenty years. Take a look at these numbers:

1999 3 percent
2000 3 percent
2001 6 percent
2002 17 percent
2003 22 percent
2004 25 percent
2005 28 percent
2006 28 percent
2007 29 percent
2008 30 percent
2009 31 percent
2010 34 percent
2011 38 percent

2012 42 percent

2013 46 percent

2014 49 percent

2015 51 percent

2016 54 percent

2017 56 percent

2018 58 percent

The percentages represent the share of physical gross merchandise sales sold on Amazon by independent third-party sellers—mostly small and medium-sized businesses—as opposed to Amazon retail's own first party sales. Third-party sales have grown from 3 percent of the total to 58 percent. To put it bluntly:

Third-party sellers are kicking our first-party butt. Badly.

And it's a high bar too because our first-party business has grown dramatically over that period, from $1.6 billion in 1999 to $117 billion this past year. The compound annual growth rate for our first-party business in that time period is 25 percent. But in that same time, third-party sales have grown from $0.1 billion to $160 billion—a compound annual growth rate of 52 percent. To provide an external benchmark, eBay's gross merchandise sales in that period have grown at a compound rate of 20 percent, from $2.8 billion to $95 billion.

Why did independent sellers do so much better selling on Amazon than they did on eBay? And why were independent sellers able to grow so much faster than Amazon's own highly organized first-party sales organization? There isn't one answer, but we do know one extremely important part of the answer:

We helped independent sellers compete against our first-party business by investing in and offering them the very best selling tools we could imagine and build. There are many such tools, including tools that help sellers manage inventory, process payments, track shipments, create reports, and sell across borders—and we're inventing more every year. But of great importance are Fulfillment by Amazon and the Prime membership program. In combination, these two programs meaningfully improved the customer experience of buying from independent sellers. With the success of these two programs now so well established, it's difficult for most people to fully appreciate today just how radical those two offerings were at the time we launched them. We invested in both of these programs at significant financial risk and after much internal debate. We had to continue investing significantly over time as we experimented with different ideas and iterations. We could not foresee with certainty what those programs would eventually look like, let alone whether they would succeed, but they were pushed forward with intuition and heart, and nourished with optimism.

Intuition, Curiosity, and the Power of Wandering

From very early on in Amazon's life, we knew we wanted to create a culture of builders—people who are curious, explorers. They like to invent. Even when they're experts, they are "fresh" with a beginner's mind. They see the way we do things as just the way we do things now. A builder's mentality helps us approach big, hard-to-solve opportunities with a humble conviction that success can come through iteration: invent, launch, reinvent, relaunch, start over, rinse, repeat, again and again. They know the path to success is anything but straight.

Sometimes (often actually) in business, you do know where you're going, and when you do, you can be efficient. Put in place a plan and execute. In contrast, wandering in business is not efficient—but it's also not random. It's guided—by hunch, gut, intuition, curiosity, and powered by a deep conviction that the prize for customers is big enough that it's worth being a little messy and tangential to find our way there. Wandering is an essential counterbalance to efficiency. You need to employ both. The outsized discoveries—the "nonlinear" ones—are highly likely to require wandering.

AWS's millions of customers range from start-ups to large enterprises, government entities to nonprofits, each looking to build better solutions for their end users. We spend a lot of time thinking about what those organizations want and what the people inside them—developers, dev managers, ops managers, CIOs, chief digital officers, chief information security officers, etc.—want.

Much of what we build at AWS is based on listening to customers. It's critical to ask customers what they want, listen carefully to their answers, and figure out a plan to provide it thoughtfully and quickly (speed matters in business!). No business could thrive without that kind of customer obsession. But it's also not enough. The biggest needle movers will be things that customers don't know to ask for. We must invent on their behalf. We have to tap into our own inner imagination about what's possible.

AWS itself—as a whole—is an example. No one asked for AWS. No one. Turns out the world was in fact ready and hungry for an offering like AWS but didn't know it. We had a hunch, followed our curiosity, took the necessary financial risks, and began building—reworking, experimenting, and iterating countless times as we proceeded.

Within AWS, that same pattern has recurred many times. For example, we invented DynamoDB, a highly scalable, low latency key-value database now used by thousands of AWS customers. And on the listening-carefully-to-customers side, we heard loudly that companies felt constrained by their commercial database options and had been unhappy with their database providers for decades— these offerings are expensive, proprietary, have high-lock-in and punitive licensing terms. We spent several years building our own database engine, Amazon Aurora, a fully managed MySQL and PostgreSQL-compatible service with the same or better durability and availability as the commercial engines, but at one-tenth of the cost. We were not surprised when this worked.

But we're also optimistic about specialized databases for specialized workloads. Over the past twenty to thirty years, companies ran most of their workloads using relational databases. The broad familiarity with relational databases among developers made this technology the go-to even when it wasn't ideal. Though suboptimal, the data set sizes were often small enough and the acceptable query latencies long enough that you could make it work. But today, many applications are storing very large amounts of data—terabytes and petabytes. And the requirements for apps have changed. Modern applications are driving the need for low latencies, real-time processing, and the ability to process millions of requests per second. It's not just key-value stores like DynamoDB, but also in-memory databases like Amazon ElastiCache, time series databases like Amazon Timestream, and ledger solutions like Amazon Quantum Ledger Database—the right tool for the right job saves money and gets your product to market faster.

We're also plunging into helping companies harness machine learning. We've been working on this for a long time, and, as with other important advances, our initial attempts to externalize some of our early internal machine learning tools were failures. It took years of wandering—experimentation, iteration, and refinement, as well as valuable insights from our customers—to enable us to find SageMaker, which launched just eighteen months ago. SageMaker removes the heavy lifting, complexity, and guesswork from each step of the machine learning process—democratizing AI. Today, thousands of customers are building machine learning models on top of AWS with SageMaker. We continue to enhance the service, including by adding new reinforcement learning capabilities. Reinforcement learning has a steep learning curve and many moving parts, which has largely put it out of reach of all but the most well-funded and technical organizations, until now. None of this would be possible without a culture of curiosity and a willingness to try totally new things on behalf of customers. And customers are responding to our customer-centric wandering and listening—AWS is now a $30 billion annual run rate business and growing fast.

Imagining the Impossible

Amazon today remains a small player in global retail. We represent a low single-digit percentage of the retail market, and there are much larger retailers in every country where we operate. And that's largely because nearly 90 percent of retail remains offline, in brick and mortar stores. For many years, we considered how we might serve customers in physical stores, but felt we needed first to invent something that would really delight customers in that environment. With Amazon Go, we had a clear vision. Get rid of the worst thing about physical retail: checkout lines. No one likes to wait in line. Instead, we imagined a store where you could walk in, pick up what you wanted, and leave.

Getting there was hard. Technically hard. It required the efforts of hundreds of smart, dedicated computer scientists and engineers around the world. We had to design and build our own proprietary cameras and shelves and invent new computer vision algorithms, including the ability to stitch together imagery from hundreds of cooperating cameras. And we had to do it in a way where the technology worked so well that it simply receded into the background, invisible. The reward has been the response from customers, who've described the experience of shopping at Amazon Go as "magical." We now have ten stores in Chicago, San Francisco, and Seattle, and are excited about the future.

Failure Needs to Scale Too

As a company grows, everything needs to scale, including the size of your failed experiments. If the size of your failures isn't growing, you're not going to be inventing at a size that can actually move the needle. Amazon will be experimenting at the right scale for a company of our size if we occasionally have multibillion-dollar failures. Of course, we won't undertake such experiments cavalierly. We will work hard to make them good bets, but not all good bets will ultimately pay out. This kind of large-scale risk taking is part of the service we as a large company can provide to our customers and to society. The good news for shareowners is that a single big winning bet can more than cover the cost of many losers.

Development of the Fire phone and Echo was started around the same time. While the Fire phone was a failure, we were able to take our learnings (as well as the developers) and accelerate our efforts building Echo and Alexa. The vision for Echo and Alexa was inspired by the *Star Trek* computer. The idea also had origins in two other arenas where we'd been building and wandering for years: machine learning and the cloud. From Amazon's early days, machine learning was an essential part of our product recommendations, and AWS gave us a front row seat to the capabilities of the cloud. After many years of development, Echo debuted in 2014, powered by Alexa, who lives in the AWS cloud.

No customer was asking for Echo. This was definitely us wandering. Market research doesn't help. If you had gone to a customer in 2013 and said "Would you like a black, always-on cylinder in your kitchen about the size of a Pringles can that you can talk to and ask questions, that also turns on your lights and plays music?" I guarantee you they'd have looked at you strangely and said, "No, thank you."

Since that first-generation Echo, customers have purchased more than one hundred million Alexa-enabled devices. Last year, we improved Alexa's ability to understand requests and answer questions by more than 20 percent, while adding billions of facts to make Alexa more knowledgeable than ever. Developers doubled the number of Alexa skills to over eighty thousand, and customers spoke to Alexa tens of billions more times in 2018 compared to 2017. The number of devices with Alexa built-in more than doubled in 2018. There are now more than 150 different products available with Alexa built-in, from headphones and PCs to cars and smart home devices. Much more to come!

One last thing before closing. As I said in the first shareholder letter more than twenty years ago, our focus is on hiring and retaining versatile and talented employees who can think like owners. Achieving that requires investing in our employees, and, as with so many other things at Amazon, we use not just analysis but also intuition and heart to find our way forward.

Last year, we raised our minimum wage to $15-an-hour for all full-time, part-time, temporary, and seasonal employees across the United States. This wage hike benefitted more than 250,000 Amazon employees, as well as over 100,000 seasonal employees who worked at Amazon sites across the country last holiday. We strongly believe that this will benefit our business as we invest in our employees. But that is not what drove the decision. We had always offered competitive wages. But we decided it was time to lead—to offer wages that went beyond competitive. We did it because it seemed like the right thing to do.

Today I challenge our top retail competitors (you know who you are!) to match our employee benefits and our $15 minimum wage. Do it! Better yet, go to $16 and throw the gauntlet back at us. It's a kind of competition that will benefit everyone.

Many of the other programs we have introduced for our employees came as much from the heart as the head. I've mentioned before the Career Choice program, which pays up to 95 percent of tuition and fees towards a certificate or diploma in qualified fields of study, leading to in-demand careers for our associates, even if those careers take them away from Amazon. More than sixteen thousand employees have now taken advantage of the program, which continues to grow. Similarly, our Career Skills program trains hourly associates in critical job skills like resume writing, how to communicate effectively, and computer basics. In October of last year, in continuation of these commitments, we signed the President's Pledge to America's Workers and announced we will be upskilling fifty thousand US employees through our range of innovative training programs.

Our investments are not limited to our current employees or even to the present. To train tomorrow's workforce, we have pledged $50 million, including through our recently announced Amazon Future Engineer program, to support STEM and CS education around the country for elementary, high school, and university students, with a particular focus on attracting more girls and minorities to these professions. We also continue to take advantage of the incredible talents of our veterans. We are well on our way to meeting our pledge to hire twenty-five thousand veterans and military spouses by 2021. And through the Amazon Technical Veterans Apprenticeship program, we are providing veterans on-the-job training in fields like cloud computing.

A huge thank-you to our customers for allowing us to serve you while always challenging us to do even better, to our shareowners for your continuing support, and to all our employees worldwide for your hard work and pioneering spirit. Teams all across Amazon are listening to customers and wandering on their behalf!

It remains Day 1.

Scale for Good

2019

To our shareowners:

One thing we've learned from the COVID-19 crisis is how important Amazon has become to our customers. We want you to know we take this responsibility seriously, and we're proud of the work our teams are doing to help customers through this difficult time.

Amazonians are working around the clock to get necessary supplies delivered directly to the doorsteps of people who need them. The demand we are seeing for essential products has been and remains high. But unlike a predictable holiday surge, this spike occurred with little warning, creating major challenges for our suppliers and delivery network. We quickly prioritized the stocking and delivery of essential household staples, medical supplies, and other critical products.

Our Whole Foods Market stores have remained open, providing fresh food and other vital goods for customers. We are taking steps to help those most vulnerable to the virus, setting aside the first hour of shopping at Whole Foods each day for seniors. We have temporarily closed Amazon Books, Amazon 4-star, and Amazon Pop Up stores because they don't sell essential products, and we offered associates from those closed stores the opportunity to continue working in other parts of Amazon.

Crucially, while providing these essential services, we are focused on the safety of our employees and contractors around the world—we are deeply grateful for their heroic work and are committed to their health and well-being. Consulting closely with medical experts and health authorities, we've made over 150 significant process changes in our operations network and Whole Foods Market stores to help teams stay healthy, and we conduct daily audits of the measures we've put into place. We've distributed face masks and implemented temperature checks at sites around the world to help protect employees and support staff. We regularly sanitize door handles, stairway handrails, lockers, elevator buttons, and touch screens, and disinfectant wipes and hand sanitizer are standard across our network.

We've also introduced extensive social distancing measures to help protect our associates. We have eliminated stand-up meetings during shifts, moved information sharing to bulletin boards, staggered break times, and spread out chairs in breakrooms. While training new hires is challenging with new distancing requirements, we continue to ensure that every new employee gets six hours of safety training. We've shifted training protocols so we don't have employees gathering in one spot, and we've adjusted our hiring processes to allow for social distancing.

A next step in protecting our employees might be regular testing of all Amazonians, including those showing no symptoms. Regular testing on a global scale, across all industries, would both help keep people safe and help get the economy back up and running. For this to work, we as a society would need vastly more testing capacity than is currently available. If every person could be tested regularly, it would make a huge difference in how we fight this virus. Those who test positive could be quarantined and cared for, and everyone who tests negative could re-enter the economy with confidence.

We've begun the work of building incremental testing capacity. A team of Amazonians—from research scientists and program managers to procurement specialists and software engineers—moved from their normal day jobs onto a dedicated team to work on this initiative. We have begun assembling the equipment we need to build our first lab and hope to start testing small numbers of our frontline employees soon. We are not sure how far we will get in the relevant timeframe, but we think it's worth trying, and we stand ready to share anything we learn.

While we explore longer-term solutions, we are also committed to helping support employees now. We increased our minimum wage through the end of April by $2 per hour in the United States, $2 per hour in Canada, £2 per hour in the United Kingdom, and €2 per hour in many European countries. And we are paying associates double our regular rate for any overtime worked—a minimum of $34 an hour—an increase from time and a half. These wage increases will cost more than $500 million, just through the end of April, and likely more than that over time. While we recognize this is expensive, we believe it's the right thing to do under the circumstances. We also established the Amazon Relief Fund—with an initial $25 million in funding—to support our independent delivery service partners and their drivers, Amazon Flex participants, and temporary employees under financial distress.

In March, we opened one hundred thousand new positions across our fulfillment and delivery network. Earlier this week, after successfully filling those roles, we announced we were creating another seventy-five thousand jobs to respond to customer demand. These new hires are helping customers who depend on us to meet their critical needs. We know that many people around the world have suffered financially as jobs are lost or furloughed. We are happy to have them on our teams until things return to normal and either their former employer can bring them back or new jobs become available. We've welcomed Joe Duffy, who joined after losing his job as a mechanic at Newark airport and learned about an opening from a friend who is an Amazon operations analyst. Dallas preschool teacher Darby Griffin joined after her school closed on March 9 and now helps manage new inventory. We're happy to have Darby with us until she can return to the classroom.

Amazon is acting aggressively to protect our customers from bad actors looking to exploit the crisis. We've removed over half a million offers from our stores due to COVID-based price gouging, and we've suspended more than six thousand selling accounts globally for violating our fair-pricing policies. Amazon turned over information about sellers we suspect engaged in price gouging of products related to COVID-19 to forty-two state attorneys general offices. To accelerate our response to price-gouging incidents, we created a special communication channel for state attorneys general to quickly and easily escalate consumer complaints to us.

Amazon Web Services is also playing an important role in this crisis. The ability for organizations to access scalable, dependable, and highly secure computing power—whether for vital health-care work, to help students continue learning, or to keep unprecedented numbers of employees online and productive from home—is critical in this situation. Hospital networks, pharmaceutical companies, and research labs are using AWS to care for patients, explore treatments, and mitigate the impacts of COVID-19 in many other ways. Academic institutions around the world are transitioning from in-person to virtual classrooms and are running on AWS to help ensure continuity of learning. And governments are leveraging AWS as a secure platform to build out new capabilities in their efforts to end this pandemic.

We are collaborating with the World Health Organization, supplying advanced cloud technologies and technical expertise to track the virus, understand the outbreak, and better contain its spread. WHO is leveraging our cloud to build large-scale data lakes, aggregate epidemiological country data, rapidly translate medical training videos into different languages, and help global health-care workers better treat patients. We are separately making a public AWS COVID-19 data lake available as a centralized repository for up-to-date and curated information related to the spread and characteristics of the virus and its associated illness so experts can access and analyze the latest data in their battle against the disease.

We also launched the AWS Diagnostic Development Initiative, a program to support customers working to bring more accurate diagnostic solutions to market for COVID-19. Better diagnostics help accelerate treatment and containment of this pandemic. We committed $20 million to accelerate this work and help our customers harness the cloud to tackle this challenge. While the program was established in response to COVID-19, we also are looking toward the future, and we will fund diagnostic research projects that have the potential to blunt future infectious disease outbreaks.

Customers around the world have leveraged the cloud to scale up services and stand up responses to COVID-19. We joined the New York City COVID-19 Rapid Response Coalition to develop a conversational agent to enable at-risk and elderly New Yorkers to receive accurate, timely information about medical and other important needs. In response to a request from the Los Angeles Unified School District to transition seven hundred thousand students to remote learning, AWS helped establish a call center to field IT questions, provide remote support, and enable staff to answer calls. We are providing cloud services to the CDC to help thousands of public health practitioners and clinicians gather data related to COVID-19 and inform response efforts. In the UK, AWS provides the cloud computing infrastructure for a project that analyzes hospital occupancy levels, emergency room capacity, and patient wait times to help the country's National Health Service decide where best to allocate resources. In Canada, OTN—one of the world's largest virtual care networks—is scaling its AWS-powered video service to accommodate a 4,000 percent spike in demand to support citizens as the pandemic continues. In Brazil, AWS will provide the São Paulo State

Government with cloud computing infrastructure to guarantee on-line classes to one million students in public schools across the state.

Following CDC guidance, our Alexa health team built an experience that lets US customers check their risk level for COVID-19 at home. Customers can ask, "Alexa, what do I do if I think I have COVID-19?" or "Alexa, what do I do if I think I have coronavirus?" Alexa then asks a series of questions about the person's symptoms and possible exposure. Based on those responses, Alexa then provides CDC-sourced guidance. We created a similar service in Japan, based on guidance from the Japanese Ministry of Health, Labor, and Welfare.

We're making it easy for customers to use Amazon.com or Alexa to donate directly to charities on the front lines of the COVID-19 crisis, including Feeding America, the American Red Cross, and Save the Children. Echo users have the option to say, "Alexa, make a donation to Feeding America COVID-19 Response Fund." In Seattle, we've partnered with a catering business to distribute seventy-three thousand meals to twenty-seven hundred elderly and medically vulnerable residents in Seattle and King County during the outbreak, and we donated eighty-two hundred laptops to help Seattle Public Schools students gain access to a device while classes are conducted virtually.

Beyond COVID

Although these are incredibly difficult times, they are an important reminder that what we do as a company can make a big difference in people's lives. Customers count on us to be there, and we are fortunate to be able to help. With our scale and ability to innovate quickly, Amazon can make a positive impact and be an organizing force for progress.

Last year, we cofounded the Climate Pledge with Christiana Figueres, the UN's former climate-change chief and founder of

Global Optimism, and became the first signatory to the pledge. The pledge commits Amazon to meet the goals of the Paris Agreement ten years early—and be net zero carbon by 2040. Amazon faces significant challenges in achieving this goal because we don't just move information around—we have extensive physical infrastructure and deliver more than ten billion items worldwide a year. And we believe if Amazon can get to net zero carbon ten years early, any company can—and we want to work together with all companies to make it a reality.

To that end, we are recruiting other companies to sign the Climate Pledge. Signatories agree to measure and report greenhouse gas emissions regularly, implement decarbonization strategies in line with the Paris Agreement, and achieve net zero annual carbon emissions by 2040. (We'll be announcing new signatories soon.)

We plan to meet the pledge, in part, by purchasing one hundred thousand electric delivery vans from Rivian—a Michigan-based producer of electric vehicles. Amazon aims to have ten thousand of Rivian's new electric vans on the road as early as 2022, and all one hundred thousand vehicles on the road by 2030. That's good for the environment, but the promise is even greater. This type of investment sends a signal to the marketplace to start inventing and developing new technologies that large, global companies need to transition to a low-carbon economy.

We've also committed to reaching 80 percent renewable energy by 2024 and 100 percent renewable energy by 2030. (The team is actually pushing to get to 100 percent by 2025 and has a challenging but credible plan to pull that off.) Globally, Amazon has eighty-six solar and wind projects that have the capacity to generate over 2,300 MW and deliver more than 6.3 million MWh of energy annually— enough to power more than 580,000 US homes.

We've made tremendous progress cutting packaging waste. More than a decade ago, we created the Frustration-Free Packaging program to encourage manufacturers to package their products in easy-to-open, 100 percent recyclable packaging that is ready to ship to customers without the need for an additional shipping box. Since 2008, this program has saved more than 810,000 tons of packaging material and eliminated the use of 1.4 billion shipping boxes.

We are making these significant investments to drive our carbon footprint to zero despite the fact that shopping online is already inherently more carbon efficient than going to the store. Amazon's sustainability scientists have spent more than three years develop- ing the models, tools, and metrics to measure our carbon footprint. Their detailed analysis has found that shopping online consistently generates less carbon than driving to a store, since a single delivery van trip can take approximately one hundred roundtrip car jour- neys off the road on average. Our scientists developed a model to compare the carbon intensity of ordering Whole Foods Market gro- ceries online versus driving to your nearest Whole Foods Market store. The study found that, averaged across all basket sizes, online grocery deliveries generate 43 percent lower carbon emissions per item compared to shopping in stores. Smaller basket sizes generate even greater carbon savings.

AWS is also inherently more efficient than the traditional in- house data center. That's primarily due to two things—higher utili- zation, and the fact that our servers and facilities are more efficient than what most companies can achieve running their own data centers. Typical single-company data centers operate at roughly 18 percent server utilization. They need that excess capacity to handle large usage spikes. AWS benefits from multitenant usage patterns and operates at far higher server utilization rates. In addition, AWS has been successful in increasing the energy efficiency of its facili- ties and equipment, for instance by using more efficient evaporative cooling in certain data centers instead of traditional air conditioning. A study by 451 Research found that AWS's infrastructure is 3.6 times more energy efficient than the median US enterprise data center surveyed. Along with our use of renewable energy, these factors en- able AWS to do the same tasks as traditional data centers with an 88 percent lower carbon footprint. And don't think we're not going to get those last twelve points—we'll make AWS 100 percent carbon free through more investments in renewable energy projects.

Leveraging Scale for Good

Over the last decade, no company has created more jobs than Amazon. Amazon directly employs 840,000 workers worldwide, including over 590,000 in the United States, 115,000 in Europe, and 95,000 in Asia. In total, Amazon directly and indirectly supports two million jobs in the United States, including 680,000-plus jobs created by Amazon's investments in areas like construction, logistics, and professional services, plus another 830,000 jobs created by small and medium-sized businesses selling on Amazon. Globally, we support nearly four million jobs. We are especially proud of the fact that many of these are entry-level jobs that give people their first opportunity to participate in the workforce.

And Amazon's jobs come with an industry-leading $15 minimum wage and comprehensive benefits. More than forty million Americans—many making the federal minimum wage of $7.25 an hour—earn less than the lowest-paid Amazon associate. When we raised our starting minimum wage to $15 an hour in 2018, it had an immediate and meaningful impact on the hundreds of thousands of people working in our fulfillment centers. We want other big employers to join us by raising their own minimum pay rates, and we continue to lobby for a $15 federal minimum wage.

We want to improve workers' lives beyond pay. Amazon provides every full-time employee with health insurance, a 401(k) plan, twenty weeks paid maternity leave, and other benefits. These are the same benefits that Amazon's most senior executives receive. And with our rapidly changing economy, we see more clearly than ever the need for workers to evolve their skills continually to keep up with technology. That's why we're spending $700 million to provide more than one hundred thousand Amazonians access to training programs, at their places of work, in high-demand fields such as health care, cloud computing, and machine learning. Since 2012, we have offered Career Choice, a prepaid tuition program for fulfillment center associates looking to move into high-demand occupations. Amazon pays up to 95 percent of tuition and fees toward a certificate or diploma in qualified fields of study, leading to enhanced employment opportunities in high-demand jobs. Since its launch, more than twenty-five thousand Amazonians have received training for in-demand occupations.

To ensure that future generations have the skills they need to thrive in a technology-driven economy, we started a program last year called Amazon Future Engineer, which is designed to educate and train low-income and disadvantaged young people to pursue careers in computer science. We have an ambitious goal: to help hundreds of thousands of students each year learn computer science and coding. Amazon Future Engineer currently funds Introduction to Computer Science and AP Computer Science classes for more than two thousand schools in underserved communities across the country. Each year, Amazon Future Engineer also gives one hundred four-year, $40,000 college scholarships to computer science students from low-income backgrounds. Those scholarship recipients also receive guaranteed, paid internships at Amazon after their first year of college. Our program in the UK funds 120 engineering apprenticeships and helps students from disadvantaged backgrounds pursue technology careers.

For now, my own time and thinking continues to be focused on COVID-19 and how Amazon can help while we're in the middle of it. I am extremely grateful to my fellow Amazonians for all the grit and ingenuity they are showing as we move through this. You can count on all of us to look beyond the immediate crisis for insights and lessons and how to apply them going forward.

Reflect on this from Theodor Seuss Geisel: "When something bad happens you have three choices. You can either let it define you, let it destroy you, or you can let it strengthen you."

Part 2

LIFE & WORK

My Gift in Life

YOU GET DIFFERENT gifts in life, and one of my great gifts is my mom and dad.

My highest admiration goes to those people—we all know some of them; I know I do—who had terrible parents but so admirably broke that cycle, pulled out of it, and made it all work. I did not have that situation. I was always loved. My parents loved me unconditionally, and, by the way, it was pretty tough for them. My mom doesn't talk about it much, but she had me when she was seventeen years old. She was a high school student in Albuquerque, New Mexico. You could ask her, but I'm pretty sure that it wasn't cool in 1964 to be a pregnant mom in high school in Albuquerque, New Mexico. In fact, my grandfather, another incredibly important figure in my life, went to bat for her because the high school wanted to kick her out. You weren't allowed to be pregnant in high school there, and my grandfather said, "You can't kick her out. It's a public school. She gets to go to school." They negotiated for a while, and the principal finally said, "Okay, she can stay and finish high school, but she can't do any extracurricular activities, and she can't have a locker." And then my grandfather, being a very wise man, said, "We'll take that deal," and so she finished high school.

My mom had me, and then she married my dad. My dad is my real dad, not my biological dad. His name is Mike. He's a Cuban immigrant. He came here as part of Operation Pedro Pan and, in fact, was put up by a Catholic mission in Wilmington, Delaware, and then got a scholarship to attend college in Albuquerque, which is where he met my mom. So I have a kind of a fairy tale story. My grandfather, possibly because my parents were so young, would take me every summer to his spectacular ranch. From age four to sixteen, I basically spent every summer working alongside him on the ranch. He was the most resourceful man. He did all his own veterinarian work. He would even make his own needles: pound the wire with an oxyacetylene torch, drill a little hole in it, sharpen it, and make a needle that he could suture up the cattle with. Some of the cattle even survived. He was a remarkable man and a huge part of all of our lives. My grandfather was like a second set of parents for me.

A Crucial Moment
at Princeton

I was born in Albuquerque but left when I was three or four, moved to Texas, and ultimately went to high school in Miami, Florida. I graduated from a big public high school, Miami Palmetto Senior High, in 1982. (Go Panthers!) There were 750 kids in my graduating class. I loved high school. I had so much fun. I lost my library privileges because I laughed too loudly in the library. I've had that laugh all my life. There was a multiyear period when my brother and sister would not see a movie with me because they thought it was too embarrassing. I don't know why I have this laugh. It's just that I laugh easily and often. Ask my mom or anybody who knows me well, and they'll say, "If Jeff's unhappy, wait five minutes since he can't maintain unhappiness." I guess I have good serotonin levels or something.

I wanted to be a theoretical physicist, and so I went to Princeton. I was a really good student, with an A+ in almost everything. I was on an honors physics track, which starts out with a hundred students, and by the time you get to quantum mechanics, it's about thirty. So I'm in quantum mechanics, probably in junior year, and I've also been taking computer science and electrical engineering classes, which I'm also enjoying. But I can't solve this one really hard partial differential equation. I'd been studying with my roommate, Joe, who also was really good at math. The two of us worked on this one homework problem for three hours and got nowhere, and we finally looked up at each other over the table at the same moment and said, "Yosanta"—the smartest guy at Princeton. We went to Yosanta's room. He is Sri Lankan and in the "facebook," which was an actual paper book at that time, and his name was three lines long because I guess in Sri Lanka, when you do something good for the king, they give you extra syllables in your name. So he had a super-long last name and was the most humble, wonderful guy. We show him this problem, and he looks at it. He stares at it for a while and says, "Cosign." I'm, like, "What do you mean," and Yosanta says, "That's the answer." And I'm, like, "That's the answer?" "Yeah, let me show you." He sits us down. He writes out three pages of detailed algebra. Everything crosses out, and the answer is cosign, and I say, "Listen, Yosanta, did you just do that in your head?" And he says, "No, that would be impossible. Three years ago I solved a very similar problem, and I was able to map this problem onto that problem, and then it was immediately obvious that the answer was cosign." That was an important moment for me because it was the very moment when I realized I was never going to be a great theoretical physicist, and so I started doing some soul-searching. In most occupations, if you're in the ninetieth percentile or above, you're going to contribute. In theoretical physics, you've got to be, like, one of the top fifty people in the world, or you're really just not helping out much. It was very clear. I saw the writing on the wall and changed my major very quickly to electrical engineering and computer science.

"We Are What We Choose"

ADDRESS TO THE PRINCETON
GRADUATING CLASS OF 2010

A S A KID, I spent my summers with my grandparents on their ranch in Texas. I helped fix windmills, vaccinate cattle, and do other chores. We also watched soap operas every afternoon, especially *Days of Our Lives*. My grandparents belonged to a Caravan Club, a group of Airstream trailer owners who travel together around the United States and Canada. And every few summers we'd join the caravan. We'd hitch up the Airstream trailer to my grandfather's car, and off we'd go in a line with three hundred other Airstream adventurers. I loved and worshipped my grandparents, and I really looked forward to these trips. On one, when I was about ten years old, I was rolling around in the big bench seat in the back of the car. My grandfather was driving. And my grandmother had the passenger seat. She smoked throughout these trips, and I hated the smell.

At that age I'd take any excuse to make estimates and do minor arithmetic—I'd calculate our gas mileage or figure out useless statistics on things like grocery spending. I'd been hearing an ad campaign about smoking. I can't remember the details, but basically the ad said that every puff of a cigarette takes some number of minutes off your life: I think it might have been two minutes per puff. At any rate, I decided to do the math for my grandmother. I estimated the number of cigarettes per day, the number of puffs per cigarette, and so on. When I was satisfied that I'd come up with a reasonable number, I poked my head into the front of the car, tapped my grandmother on the shoulder, and proudly proclaimed, "At two minutes per puff, you've taken nine years off your life!"

I have a vivid memory of what happened, and it was not what I anticipated. I expected to be applauded for my cleverness and arithmetic skills: "Jeff, you're so smart. You had to have made some tricky estimates, figure out the number of minutes in a year, and do some division." That's not what happened. Instead, my grandmother burst into tears. I sat in the backseat and did not know what to do. While my grandmother sat crying, my grandfather, who had been driving in silence, pulled over onto the shoulder of the highway. He got out of the car and came around and opened my door and waited for me to follow. Was I in trouble? My grandfather was a highly intelligent, quiet man. He had never said a harsh word to me, and maybe this was to be the first time. Or maybe he would ask that I get back in the car and apologize to my grandmother. I had no experience in this realm with my grandparents and no way to gauge what the consequences might be. We stopped beside the trailer. My grandfather looked at me, and after a bit of silence, he gently and calmly said, "Jeff, one day you'll understand that it's harder to be kind than clever."

What I want to talk to you about today is the difference between gifts and choices. Cleverness is a gift; kindness is a choice. Gifts are easy—they're given, after all. Choices can be hard. You can seduce yourself with your gifts if you're not careful, and if you do, it'll probably be to the detriment of your choices.

This is a group with many gifts. I'm sure one of your gifts is the gift of a smart and capable brain. I'm confident that's the case because admission is competitive, and if there weren't some signs that you're clever, the dean of admission wouldn't have let you in.

Your smarts will come in handy because you will travel in a land of marvels. We humans—plodding as we are—will astonish ourselves. We'll invent ways to generate clean energy and a lot of it. Atom by atom, we'll assemble tiny machines that will enter cell walls and make repairs. This month comes the extraordinary but also inevitable news that we've synthesized life. In the coming years we'll not only synthesize it, but we'll also engineer it to specifications. I believe you'll even see us understand the human brain. Jules Verne, Mark Twain, Galileo, Newton—all the curious from the ages would have wanted to be alive most of all right now. As a civilization, we will have so many gifts, just as you as individuals have so many individual gifts as you sit before me.

How will you use these gifts? And will you take pride in your gifts or pride in your choices?

I got the idea to start Amazon sixteen years ago. I came across the fact that web usage was growing at 2,300 percent per year. I'd never seen or heard of anything that grew that fast, and the idea of building an online bookstore with millions of titles—something that simply couldn't exist in the physical world—was very exciting to me. I had just turned thirty years old, and I'd been married for a year. I told my wife, MacKenzie, that I wanted to quit my job and go do this crazy thing that probably wouldn't work since most start-ups don't, and I wasn't sure what would happen after that. MacKenzie (also a Princeton grad and sitting here in the second row) told me I should go for it. As a young boy, I'd been a garage inventor. I'd invented an automatic gate closer out of cement-filled tires, a solar cooker that didn't work very well out of an umbrella and tinfoil, and baking-pan alarms to entrap my siblings. I'd always wanted to be an inventor, and she wanted me to follow my passion.

I was working at a financial firm in New York City with a bunch of very smart people, and I had a brilliant boss who I much admired. I went to my boss and told him I wanted to start a company selling books on the Internet. He took me on a long walk in Central Park, listened carefully to me, and finally said, "That sounds like a really good idea, but it would be an even better idea for someone who didn't already have a good job." That logic made some sense to me, and he convinced me to think about it for forty-eight hours before making a final decision. Seen in that light, it really was a difficult choice, but ultimately I decided I had to give it a shot. I didn't think I'd regret trying and failing. And I suspected I would always be haunted by a decision to not try at all. After much consideration, I took the less safe path to follow my passion, and I'm proud of that choice.

Tomorrow, in a very real sense, your life—the life you author from scratch on your own—begins.

How will you use your gifts? What choices will you make?

Will inertia be your guide, or will you follow your passions?

Will you follow dogma, or will you be original?

Will you choose a life of ease, or a life of service and adventure?

Will you wilt under criticism, or will you follow your convictions?

Will you bluff it out when you're wrong, or will you apologize?

Will you guard your heart against rejection, or will you act when you fall in love?

Will you play it safe, or will you be a little bit swashbuckling?

When it's tough, will you give up, or will you be relentless?

Will you be a cynic, or will you be a builder?

Will you be clever at the expense of others, or will you be kind?

I will hazard a prediction. When you are eighty years old and, in a quiet moment of reflection, narrating for only yourself the most personal version of your life story, the telling that will be most compact and meaningful will be the series of choices you have made. In the end, we are our choices. Build yourself a great story. Thank you, and good luck!

Resourcefulness

MY BROTHER AND I had a very fortunate childhood. We got to spend a lot of time with our grandparents. You learn different things from grandparents than you do from parents. It's just a very different relationship. I spent all my summers from ages four to sixteen on my grandfather's ranch. He was incredibly self-reliant. If you're in the middle of nowhere, in a rural area, you don't pick up the phone and call somebody when something breaks. You fix it yourself. As a kid, I got to see him solve all these problems himself.

My grandfather once bought a used D6 Caterpillar for $5,000. It was an enormous bargain; it should have cost way more but was so cheap because it was completely broken. The transmission was stripped. The hydraulics didn't work. And so we spent basically a whole summer repairing it. Giant gears would arrive by mail order from Caterpillar. We couldn't even move the gears. The first thing my grandfather did was build a crane to move them. That's self-reliance and resourcefulness.

He was a careful, conservative, quiet, and introverted sort of person, not prone to crazy acts. One day he was all by himself at the main gate of the ranch. And he forgot to put the car in park. When he got to the gate, he noticed the car was slowly rolling down to the gate. He thought, "This is fantastic. I have just enough time to unlatch the gate, throw the gate open, and the car is going to drive right through, and it'll be wonderful." He almost got the gate unlatched when the car hit the gate and caught his thumb between the gate and the fence post, stripping all the flesh off his thumb. It was hanging there by a tiny little thread.

He was so angry at himself that he ripped that piece of flesh off and threw it in the brush, got back in the car, and drove himself to the emergency room in Dilley, Texas, sixteen miles away. And when he got there, they said, "This is great. We can reattach that thumb. Where is it?" He said, "Oh, I threw it in the brush." They drove back with the nurses and everybody. And they looked for hours for the thumb, and they never found that piece of flesh—something had probably eaten it. They took him back to the emergency room and said, "Look, you are going to have a skin graft for that. We can sew your thumb to your stomach and leave it there for six weeks. That's the best way to do it. Or we can just cut a skin graft from your butt and suture it on, and it won't ever be as good, but the advantage is your thumb won't be sewn to your stomach for six weeks." And he said, "I'll take option two. Just do the skin graft from my butt." That's what they did. It was very successful, and his thumb worked fine. But the funniest thing about this story is that I have incredibly vivid memories—we all do—of him, and definitely his mornings were completely ritualized. He would wake up, eat breakfast cereal, read the newspaper, and shave with an electric razor for a really long time. For like fifteen minutes. When he was done shaving his face with that razor, he would take two quick passes over his thumb because his thumb grew butt hair. Which, by the way, did not bother him at all.

The whole point of moving things forward is that you run into problems, failures, things that don't work. You need to back up and try again. Each one of those times when you have a setback, you get back up and try again. You're using resourcefulness; you're using self-reliance; you're trying to invent your way out of a box. We have tons of examples at Amazon where we've had to do this. We've failed so many times—I think of this as a great place to fail. We're good at it. We've had so much practice.

To give you one example: Many years ago we wanted a third-party selling business because we knew we could add selection to the store. We started Amazon Auctions. Nobody came. Then we opened this thing called zShops, which was fixed-price auctions, and again nobody came. Each one of these failures was like a year or a year and a half long. We finally came across this idea of putting the third-party selection on the same product-detail pages as our own retail inventory. We called this Marketplace, and it started working right away. That resourcefulness of trying new things, figuring things out— what do customers really want?—pays off in everything. It pays off even in your daily life. How do you help your children? What's the right thing?

Even when our kids were four, we would let them use sharp knives, and when they were seven or eight, we would let them use certain power tools. My wife, much to her credit, has this great saying: "I would much rather have a kid with nine fingers than a resourceless kid," which is a great attitude about life.

Why I Went from
a Hedge Fund to
Selling Books

A FTER GRADUATING FROM Princeton, I went to New York City and ended up working at a quantitative hedge fund, D. E. Shaw and Co., run by David Shaw. There were only thirty people at the company when I started and about three hundred when I left. David is one of the most brilliant people I've ever met. I learned so much from him and used a lot of his ideas and principles on things like HR and recruiting and what kind of people to hire when I started Amazon.

In 1994 very, very few people had heard of the internet. It was used at that time mostly by scientists and physicists. We used it a little bit at D. E. Shaw for some things but not much, and I came across the fact that the web—the World Wide Web—was growing at something like 2,300 percent a year. Anything growing that fast, even if it's baseline usage today is tiny, is going to be big. I concluded that I should come up with a business idea based on the internet and then let the internet grow around it and keep working to improve it. So I made a list of products I might sell online. I started ranking them, and I picked books because books are super unusual in one respect: there are more items in the book category than in any other category. There are three million different books in print around the world at any given time. The biggest bookstores had only 150,000 titles. So the founding idea of Amazon was to build a universal selection of books in print. That's what I did: I hired a small team, and we built the software. I moved to Seattle because the largest book warehouse in the world at that time was nearby in a town called Roseberg, Oregon, and also because of the recruiting pool available from Microsoft.

When I told my boss, David Shaw, that I was going to do this thing, I went on a long walk with him in Central Park, and he said finally, after a lot of listening, "You know what, Jeff, this is a really good idea. I think you're onto a good idea here, but this would be a better idea for somebody who didn't already have a good job." That actually made so much sense to me, and he convinced me to think about it for two days before making a final decision. It was one of those decisions that I made with my heart and not my head, not wanting to pass up a great opportunity. When I'm eighty, I want to have minimized the number of regrets that I have in my life, and most of our regrets are acts of omission, things we didn't try, the path untraveled. Those are the things that haunt us.

At first I had to go deliver the books to the post office myself. I don't still deliver, but I was doing that for years. In the first month I was packing boxes on my hands and knees on the hard cement floors. I said to the person kneeling next to me, "You know, we need kneepads because this is killing my knees," and he said, "What we need are packing tables"—the most brilliant idea I'd ever heard. The next day I went and bought packing tables and doubled our productivity.

The name *Amazon* comes from Earth's biggest river, a reference to "Earth's biggest selection." The first name was Cadabra. When I was driving to Seattle, I wanted to hit the ground running. I wanted to have a company incorporated and have a bank account set up. I called a friend, and he recommended his lawyer, who was actually his divorce attorney. But he incorporated the company for me, set up bank accounts, and said, "I need to know what name you want the company to have for the incorporation papers." Over the phone I said, "Cadabra"—like "abracadabra." And he responded, "Cadaver?" And I said, "Okay, that's not going to work, but go ahead with Cadabra for now and I'll change it." And so, around three months later, I changed it to Amazon.

After books we started selling music and then videos. Then I got smart and emailed a thousand randomly selected customers and asked them, besides the things we already sold, what would they like to see us sell. And that answer came back incredibly long-tailed. They answered the question with whatever they were looking for at that moment. So I remember one of the answers was "I wish you sold windshield wiper blades because I really need windshield wiper blades." I thought to myself, "We can sell anything this way." So then we launched electronics and toys and, over time, many other categories.

At the pinnacle of the internet bubble our stock peaked somewhere around $113, and then after the internet bubble burst, in less than a year our stock went down to $6. My annual shareholder letter for 2000, as noted in Part I, starts with a one-word sentence: "Ouch."

That whole period is very interesting because the stock is not the company, and the company is not the stock, and so, as I watched the stock fall from $113 to $6, I was also watching all of our internal business metrics—number of customers, profit per unit, defects—everything you can imagine (see the 2000 letter for details). Every single thing about the business was getting better and fast. And so, as the stock price was going the wrong way, everything inside the company was going the right way, and we didn't need to go back to the capital markets. We already had the money we needed, so we just needed to continue to progress.

During that era I was on television with Tom Brokaw. He pulled together half a dozen internet entrepreneurs from that era and was interviewing all of us. Tom is now one of my good friends, but at the time he turned to me and said, "Mr. Bezos, can you even spell profit?" And I said, "Sure, P-R-O-P-H-E-T," and he burst out laughing. People always accused us of selling dollar bills for ninety cents, and I said, "Look, anybody can do that and grow revenues." That's not what we were doing. We always had positive gross margins. It's a fixed-cost business, and so I could see from the internal metrics that, at a certain volume level, we would cover our fixed costs, and the company would be profitable.

Finding the Root Cause

I'M A CUSTOMER of Amazon and sometimes have problems with an order. I treat these problems the same way I treat a problem that I hear about from a customer—as an opportunity to improve. My email address, jeff@amazon.com, is well known. I keep that address and read my emails, though I don't see every single one anymore because I get too many. But I see a lot of them, and I use my curiosity to pick out certain emails. For example, I'll get one from a customer about a defect. We've done something wrong. That's usually why people are writing us—not always, but usually they're writing us because we've screwed up their order somehow. So I'm looking at an email, and for some reason something may seem a little odd about it. So I'll ask the Amazon team to do a case study and find the real root cause or causes—and then do real root fixes. So then, when you fix it, you're not just fixing it for that one customer. You're fixing it for every customer, and that process is a gigantic part of what we do. So if I have a failed order or a bad customer experience, I treat it just like that.

Creating Wealth

I T'S SOMETHING PEOPLE are naturally curious about, but I have never sought the title of "world's richest man." I was fine being the second-wealthiest person in the world. I would much rather be known as inventor Jeff Bezos or entrepreneur Jeff Bezos or father Jeff Bezos. Those kinds of things are much more meaningful to me, and it's an output measure. If you look at the financial success of Amazon and the stock, I own 16 percent of Amazon. Amazon's worth roughly $1 trillion.* That means that over twenty years we have built $840 billion of wealth for other people, and that's really what we've done from a financial point of view. We've built $840 billion of wealth for other people, and that's great. That's how it should be. You know, I believe so powerfully in the ability of entrepreneurial capitalism and free markets to solve so many of the world's problems. Not all of them, but so many of them.

---

*As of September 13, 2018. Amazon's value, as of this writing (July 6, 2020), is now $1.44 trillion, of which I own 11 percent.

The Idea for Prime

MOST OF THE inventing we do at Amazon goes like this: some-body has an idea, other people improve the idea, other people come up with objections for why it can never work, and then we solve those objections. It's a very fun process. We were always wondering what a loyalty program could be, and then a junior software engineer came up with the idea that we could offer people a kind of all-you-can-eat buffet of fast, free shipping.

When the finance team modeled that idea, the results were horrifying. Shipping is expensive, but customers love free shipping.

You have to use heart and intuition. There has to be risk taking. You have to have instinct. All the good decisions have to be made that way. You do it with a group. You do it with great humility because, by the way, getting it wrong isn't that bad. That's the other thing. We've made mistakes, doozies like the Fire Phone and many other things that just didn't work out. I won't list all of our failed experiments, but the big winners pay for thousands of failed experiments.

So we tried Prime, and it was very expensive at the beginning. It cost us a lot of money because what happens when you offer a free all-you-can-eat buffet? Who shows up to the buffet first? The heavy eaters. It's scary. It's like, oh my god, did I really say as many prawns as you can eat? And so that is what happened, but we could see the trend lines. We could see all kinds of customers were coming, and they appreciated that service, so that's what led to the success of Prime.

Thinking Three Years Out

I LIKE TO PUTTER in the morning. I get up early. I go to bed early. I like to read the newspaper. I like to have coffee. I like to have breakfast with my kids before they go to school. So my puttering time is very important to me. That's why I set my first meeting for ten o'clock. I like to do my high-IQ meetings before lunch. Anything that's going to be really mentally challenging is a ten o'clock meeting because by 5 P.M., I'm, like, I can't think more about this issue today. Let's try this again tomorrow at 10 A.M. Then on to eight hours of sleep. I prioritize sleep unless I'm traveling in different time zones. Sometimes getting eight hours is impossible, but I am very focused on it, and I need eight hours. I think better. I have more energy. My mood is better. And think about it: As a senior executive, what do you really get paid to do? You get paid to make a small number of high-quality decisions. Your job is not to make thousands of decisions every day. So let's say I slept six hours a day, or let's go really crazy and say I slept four hours a day. I'd get four so-called productive hours back. So if before I had, say, twelve hours of productive time during any waking day, now all of a sudden I have twelve plus four—I have sixteen productive hours. So I have 33 percent more time to make decisions. If I was going to make, say, one hundred decisions, I can now make thirty-three more. Is that really worth it if the quality of those decisions might be lower because you're tired or grouchy or any number of things? Now, it's different if the company is a start-up. When Amazon was a hundred people, it was a different story, but Amazon's not a start-up company, and all of our senior executives operate the same way I do. They work in the future. They live in the future. None of the people who report to me should really be focused on the current quarter. When I have a good quarterly conference call with Wall Street, people will stop me and say, "Congratulations on your quarter," and I say, "Thank you," but what I'm really thinking is that quarter was baked three years ago. Right now I'm working on a quarter that's going to reveal itself in 2023 sometime, and that's what you need to be doing. You need to be thinking two or three years in advance, and if you are, then why do I need to make a hundred decisions today? If I make, like, three good decisions a day, that's enough, and they should just be as high quality as I can make them. Warren Buffet says he's good if he makes three good decisions a year, and I really believe that.

Where the Idea of Amazon Web Services Came From

W̲E̲ ̲W̲O̲R̲K̲E̲D̲ ̲O̲N̲ Amazon Web Services (AWS) behind the scenes for a long time, then finally launched it. AWS has become a very large company by reinventing the way companies buy computation. Traditionally, if you were a company and needed computation, you would build a data center, and you'd fill that data center with servers, and you'd have to upgrade the operating systems of those servers and keep everything running, and so on. None of that added any value to what the business was doing. It was kind of a price-of-admission, undifferentiated heavy lifting.

At Amazon we were doing just that: building data centers for ourselves. We saw it was a tremendous waste of effort between our applications engineers and our networking engineers, the ones who run the data centers, because they were having lots of meetings on all these non-value-added tasks. We said, "Look, what we can do is develop a set of hardened application program interfaces–APIs– that allow these two groups, the applications engineers and the networking engineers, to have roadmap meetings instead of these fine-grained meetings." We wanted to build in a service-oriented architecture, where all of our services were available in hardened APIs that were well documented enough that anybody could use them.

As soon as we hatched that plan for ourselves, it became immediately obvious that every company in the world was going to want this. What really surprised us was that thousands of developers flocked to these APIs without much promotion or fanfare from Amazon. And then a business miracle that never happens happened—the greatest piece of business luck in the history of business, so far as I know. We faced no like-minded competition for seven years. It's unbelievable. When I launched Amazon.com in 1995, Barnes & Noble then launched Barnesandnoble.com and entered the market two years later in 1997. Two years later is very typical if you invent something new. We launched Kindle; Barnes & Noble launched Nook two years later. We launched Echo; Google launched Google Home two years later. When you pioneer, if you're lucky, you get a two-year head start. Nobody gets a seven-year head start, and so that was unbelievable. I think that the big, established enterprise software companies did not see Amazon as a credible enterprise software company, so we had this long runway to build this incredible, feature-rich product and service that is just so far ahead, and the team doesn't let up. This team, led by Andy Jassy, is innovating on the product side so rapidly, and they're running everything so well. I'm very proud of them.

Alexa, AI, and
Machine Learning

ALEXA IS THE agent in the cloud, running on the internet. Echo is the device with a multitude of microphones so it can do far-field voice recognition. From the time we started working on it in 2012, our vision was that—in the long term—it would become the *Star Trek* computer. You could ask it anything—ask it to do things for you, ask it to find things for you—and it would be easy to converse with in a very natural way.

Working on Alexa and Echo was very challenging from a technical point of view. There are thousands of people working on Echo and Alexa, with teams in many different locations, including Cambridge, Massachusetts; Berlin; and Seattle.

With Echo there were several different things that had to get solved. One of the key insights we had when we started planting that seed for Echo was an always-on device, a device that was plugged into wall power, so you didn't need to charge it. It could sit in your bedroom or in your kitchen or in your living room and play music for you, answer questions, and ultimately even be the way you might control some of your home systems, like lighting and temperature control. Just saying, "Alexa, please turn the temperature up two de-grees" or "Alexa, turn off all the lights" is a very natural way of in-teracting in that kind of environment. Before Echo and Alexa, the primary way people interacted with their home automation system was bad: an app on their phone. If you want to control your lights, it's very inconvenient if you need to find your phone, take it out, open a particular app, and find the right screen to control the lights on that app.

The devices team has just done an amazing job, and there's so much progress still to come. We have a fantastic road map for Echo and Alexa. We have a big third-party ecosystem now of other com-panies who've built what we call *skills* for Alexa, so it's kind of ex-panding what Alexa can do.

We—as humanity, as a civilization, as a technological civilization—are still quite a ways away from making anything as magical and amazing as the *Star Trek* computer. That has been a dream for so long, kind of a science-fiction scenario. The things we're solving with machine learning today are extraordinary, and we really are at a tipping point where the progress is accelerating. I think we're en-tering a golden age of machine learning and artificial intelligence. But we're still a long way away from being able to have machines do things the way humans do things.

Human-like intelligence is still pretty mysterious, even to the most advanced AI researchers. If you think about how humans learn, we're incredibly data efficient. So when we train something like Al-exa to recognize natural language, we use millions of data points. And you have to collect what's called a ground-truth database. It's a huge, expensive effort to collect this ground-truth database that becomes the training set that Alexa learns from.

If today you are designing and building a machine-learning system for a self-driving car, you need millions of driving miles of data for that car to learn how to drive. Humans learn incredibly efficiently. Humans do not need to drive millions of miles before we learn how to drive. We're probably doing something called "transfer learning" in the parlance of the machine-learning field.

Humans have already learned so many different skills, and we're able to map those skills onto new skills in a very efficient way. The AlphaGo program that recently just beat the world Go champion played millions of games of Go. The human champion has played thousands of games of Go, not millions. And they're almost at the same level, the human champion and the computer program. Plus, the human is doing something fundamentally different—we know because we are so power efficient.

I don't remember the exact figure, but AlphaGo is one example that uses thousands and thousands of watts of power. I think it's over one thousand servers running in parallel. And Lee Se-dol, the human champion, uses about fifty watts. Somehow we're doing these unbelievably complex calculations incredibly power efficiently—we're data efficient and power efficient. So when it comes to AI, we in the machine-learning community have a lot to learn.

But that's what makes it such an exciting field. We're solving unbelievably complex problems and not just in natural language and machine vision but also in some cases even the fusion of those two.

Privacy organizations take claims about privacy invasion related to devices or services and attempt to reenact the invasion claims. It's actually pretty easy for privacy organizations to do this, and they do it all the time. They reverse-engineer devices to see if their privacy claims are true. And that's a very good behavior, and I'm grateful for all those privacy organizations that do that. And they have uncovered honest mistakes that companies have made—sometimes maybe companies just weren't careful enough.

Our device is not transmitting anything to the cloud until it hears the wake word, "Alexa." And when it hears the wake word "Alexa," the ring on the top lights up. When the ring is lit, the device is sending what you say to the cloud. It has to do that because we need access to all of the data in the cloud in order to be able to do the full range of things that Alexa can do—check the weather for you and so on.

Hacking is one of the great issues of our age, one that as a society and a civilization we have to globally figure out. And some of the solutions will become laws. Some of it is nation–states doing things that you wouldn't want them to do, and it's not clear at all how that's going to be controlled.

With most devices and the technologies we have today, nation–states can easily listen in on any conversation by bouncing a laser beam off one of your windows in your home, or they can put a piece of malware on your phone and turn all the microphones on. A typical high-end phone today has four microphones. So we're going to have to figure out as a society that it's probably easier to control certain institutions like the FBI because we can come together and decide what the rules should be, what the laws should be, and how courts should enforce them. But when it comes to nation–states cyberhacking and so on, I consider it an unsolved issue. I don't know what we're going to do.

I don't know the answer to the question of whether an internet-connected society can ever be made really secure. We've lived with these technologies for a long time. People want to carry a phone around, and I think that the phone phenomenon is here to stay. And that phone is completely controlled by software. It has multiple microphones on it. The microphones are controlled by software. The radio in that phone can transmit the data anywhere in the world.

And so the technical capability is there to turn any mobile phone into a listening device surreptitiously. With Alexa, the team made a very interesting and, I think, noteworthy decision. I hope other companies might emulate this decision—to include a mute button that turns the microphone off on the Echo. When you press the mute button, it and the ring turns red, and that red light is connected to the microphone with analog electronics. So it's actually impossible, when that red light is on, for the microphones to come on. You can't do that remotely through hacking. But phones are not like that.

Physical Stores and
Whole Foods

WE HAVE BEEN very interested in physical stores for years, but I always said we were only interested in having a differentiated offering, something that's not me-too, because that space—physical stores—is so well served. If we had a me-too product offering, I knew it wasn't going to work. Our culture is much better at pioneering and inventing, and so we have to have something that's different. And that's what Amazon Go is. It's completely different. The Amazon Bookstore, completely different. And we have ideas about how to merge Prime and Whole Foods to make Whole Foods a very differentiated experience.

Amazon buys a lot of companies. Usually they're much smaller than Whole Foods, but we buy a bunch of companies every year. When I meet with the entrepreneur who founded the company, I'm always trying to figure out one thing first and foremost: Is this person a missionary or a mercenary? The mercenaries are trying to flip their stock. The missionaries love their product or their service and love their customers, and they're trying to build a great service. By the way, the great paradox here is that it's usually the missionaries who make more money, and you can tell really quickly just by talking to people. Whole Foods is a missionary company, and John Mackey, the founder, is a missionary guy. And so what we're going to be able to do is take some of our resources, some of our technological know-how, and expand the Whole Foods mission. They have a great mission, which is to bring organic, nourishing food to everybody, and we have a lot to bring to that table in terms of resources but also in terms of operational excellence and technological know-how.

Buying the *Washington Post*

I WAS NOT LOOKING for a newspaper and had no intention of buying a newspaper. I had never thought about the idea. It wasn't like a childhood dream. My friend Don Graham, whom I've known for over twenty years, approached me through an intermediary and wanted to know if I would be interested in buying the *Washington Post*. I sent back word that I would not because I didn't really know anything about newspapers.

Don, however, over a series of conversations, convinced me that was unimportant because the *Washington Post* already had so much internal talent who understood newspapers. What they needed was somebody who had an understanding of the internet, and so that was the first thing. That's kind of how it got started, and then I did some soul-searching. And my decision-making process was definitely intuitive and not analysis driven. The financial situation of the *Washington Post* at that time, in 2013, was very upside down. It was a fixed-cost business and had lost a lot of revenue over the previous five or six years, not through any fault of the people working there or of the leadership team. The paper had been managed very, very well. The problem was a secular one, not cyclical. The internet was just eroding all of the traditional advantages that local newspapers enjoyed. It's a profound problem across local newspapers all around the country and the world. So I had to do some soul-searching, and I asked myself whether this was something I wanted to get involved in. If I was going to do it, I was going to put some heart into it and some work into it, and I decided I would only do that if I really believed it was an important institution. I said to myself, "If this were a financially upside-down salty snack food company, the answer would be no." I started thinking about the *Post* as an important institution, the newspaper in the capital city of the most important country in the world. The *Washington Post* has an incredibly important role to play in this democracy. There's just no doubt in my mind about that.

And so, as soon as I had passed through that gate, I only had one more gate I had to go through before telling Don yes. I wanted to be really open with myself, to look in the mirror and think about the company and be sure I was optimistic that it could work. If it were hopeless, that would not be something I would get involved in. I looked at the *Post*'s situation, and I was super optimistic, but it needed to be transitioned into a national and a global publication. There's one gift the internet brings newspapers. It destroys almost everything, but it brings one gift, and that is free global distribution. In the old days of paper newspapers, you would need to build printing plants everywhere. Your logistics operations, to have a truly global newspaper or even a really national newspaper, meant super-expensive, heavy-capital-expenditure investments. That's why so few papers actually became national or global. But today, with the internet, you get that gift of free distribution. So we had to take advantage of that gift, and that was the basic strategy. We had to switch from a business model where we made a lot of money per reader with a relatively small number of readers to a tiny bit of money per reader with a very large number of readers, and that's the transition we made. I'm pleased to report that the *Post* is profitable today. The newsroom is growing. Marty Baron, who leads the newsroom, is killing it. I think he's the best editor in the newspaper business. We have Fred Ryan, the publisher, and Fred Hyatt on the editorial page.

Trust

THE WAY YOU earn trust, the way you develop a reputation is by doing hard things well over and over and over. The reason, for example, that the US military, in all polls, has such high credibility and reputation is because, over and over again, decade after decade, it has done hard things well.

It really is that simple. It's also that complicated. It's not easy to do hard things well, but that's how you earn trust. And trust, of course, is an overloaded word. It means so many different things. It's integrity, but it's also competence. It's doing what you said you were going to do—and delivering. And so we deliver billions of packages every year; we say we're going to do that, and then we actually do it. And it's also taking controversial stances. People like it when you say, "No, we're not going to do it that way. I know you want us to do it that way, but we're not going to." And even if they disagree, they might say, "We kind of respect that, though. They know who they are."

It is also helpful to have clarity. If we are clear that we are going to do this and we aren't going to do that, then people can opt in or opt out. They can say, "Well, if that's Amazon's position or Blue Origin's position or AWS's position on something, then I don't want to be part of that." And that's okay. We live in a big democracy with lots of opinions, and I want to live in that world. I want to live in a place where people can disagree. What I want, too, is to live in a place where people can disagree and still work together. I don't want to lose that. People are entitled to their opinions, but it is the job of a senior leadership team to say no.

One of the things that's happening inside technology companies is that there are groups of employees who, for example, think that technology companies should not work with the Department of Defense. In my view, if big tech is going to turn its back on the Department of Defense, this country is in trouble. That just can't happen. And so the senior leadership team needs to say to people, "Look, I understand these are emotional issues. That's okay, and we don't have to agree on everything, but this is how we're going to do it. We are going to support the Department of Defense. This country is important. It is still."

I do know that people are very emotional about this issue and have different opinions, but there is truth in the world. We are the good guys. I really believe that. And I know it's complicated. But the question is: Do you want a strong national defense, or don't you? I think you do. And so we have to support that.

We all want to be on the side of civilization. It's not exclusively only in the United States. What kind of civilization do you want? Do you want freedom? Do you want democracy? These are big principles that supersede the other kinds of questions. And so that's where you should go back to.

Work-Life Harmony

I TEACH LEADERSHIP CLASSES at Amazon for our most senior executives. I also speak to interns. Across the spectrum I get the question about work-life balance all the time. I don't even like the phrase "work-life balance." I think it's misleading. I like the phrase "work-life harmony." I know if I am energized at work, happy at work, feeling like I'm adding value, part of a team, whatever energizes you, that makes me better at home. It makes me a better husband, a better father. Likewise, if I'm happy at home, it makes me a better employee, a better boss. There may be crunch periods when it's about the number of hours in a week. But that's not the real thing. Usually it's about whether you have energy. Is your work depriving you of energy, or is your work generating energy for you?

Everybody knows people who fall into one of two camps. You're in a meeting, and the person comes in the room. Some people come into the meeting and add energy to the meeting. Other people come into the meeting, and the whole meeting just deflates. Those people drain energy from the meeting. And you have to decide which of those kinds of people you are going to be. It's the same thing at home.

It's a flywheel, a circle, not a balance. That's why that metaphor is so dangerous, because it implies there's a strict trade-off. You could be out of work, have all the time in the world for your family, but be really depressed and demoralized about your work situation, and your family wouldn't want to be anywhere near you. They would wish you would take a vacation from them. It's not about the number of hours, not primarily. I suppose if you went crazy with one hundred hours a week or something, maybe there are limits, but I've never had a problem, and I suppose it's because both sides of my life give me energy. That's what I recommend to both interns and executives.

Recruiting Talent

Do You Want Mercenaries or Missionaries?

WE PAY VERY competitive compensation at Amazon, but we have not created that kind of country club culture where you get free massages and whatever the perks of the moment are. And I have always had a bit of skepticism about those kinds of perks because I always worry that people will stay with a company for the wrong reasons. You want people to stay for the mission. You don't want mercenaries at your company. You want missionaries.

Missionaries care about the mission. It's actually not very complicated. And you can confuse people with free massages. Like, "Oh, I don't really like the mission here, but I love the free massages."

How do you hire great people and keep them from leaving? By giving them, first of all, a great mission—something that has real purpose, that has meaning. People want meaning in their lives. And this is a giant advantage that the US military has because its people have a real mission. They have meaning. And that is huge. And so that's a big recruiting advantage.

But you can drive great people away—for example, by making the speed of decision making really slow. Why would great people stay in an organization where they can't get things done? They look around after a while, and they're, like, "Look, I love the mission, but I can't get my job done because our speed of decision making is too slow." So large companies like Amazon need to worry about that.

Decisions

THERE ARE WAYS to increase the speed of decision making, and it's super important. If I were to be so bold as to advise other senior leaders, I would say one of the things to watch out for—I see it at Amazon—is junior executives modeling senior executives in their decision making. And that's normal. But you're always looking up at the senior people and modeling. And a lot of it is even subconscious. The problem with that modeling is that it may not take into account the fact that there are different types of decisions.

There are two types of decisions. There are decisions that are irreversible and highly consequential; we call them one-way doors, or Type 2 decisions. They need to be made slowly and carefully. I often find myself at Amazon acting as the chief slowdown officer: "Whoa, I want to see that decision analyzed seventeen more ways because it's highly consequential and irreversible." The problem is that most decisions aren't like that. Most decisions are two-way doors.

You can make the decision, and you step through. It turns out to have been the wrong decision; you can back up. And what happens in large organizations—not in start-up companies but in large organizations—is that all decisions end up using the heavyweight process that is really intended only for irreversible, highly consequential decisions. And that's a disaster. When there's a decision that needs to be made, you need to ask, "Is it a one-way door or a two-way door?" If it's a two-way door, make the decision with a small team or even one high-judgment individual. Make the decision. If it's wrong, it's wrong. You'll change it. But if it's a one-way door, analyze it five different ways. Be careful, because that is where slow is smooth and smooth is fast.

You do not want to make one-way-door decisions quickly. You want to get consensus or at least drive a lot of thought and debate.

What can also really speed up decision making, in addition to asking whether a decision involves a one-way or two-way door, is teaching the principle of disagreeing and committing. So you've got passionate missionaries, which you need to have. Everybody cares, and if you're not careful, the decision process can basically become a war of attrition. Whoever has the most stamina will win; eventually the other party, with the opposite opinion, will just capitulate: "Okay, I'm exhausted. We'll do it your way."

That is the worst decision-making process in the world. It leaves everybody demoralized, and you also get a kind of random result. A much better approach is for the more senior person to escalate to even more senior leaders. Controversial decisions need to be escalated quickly. You can't let two junior people argue for a year and exhaust themselves. You have to teach those junior people.

When your team is really at loggerheads, escalate—and escalate fast. And then you, as the more senior person, hear the various points of view, and you say, "Look, none of us knows what the right decision is here, but I want you to gamble with me. I want you to disagree and commit. We're going to do it this way. But I really want you to disagree and commit."

And here's the important part: Sometimes this disagreement happens between the more senior person and a subordinate. The subordinate really wants to do it one way, and the senior person really thinks it should be done a different way. And it's often the case that the more senior person should disagree and commit. I disagree and commit all the time. I'll debate something for an hour or a day or a week. And I'll say, "You know what? I really disagree with this, but you have more ground truth than I do. We're going to do it your way. And I promise I will never tell you I told you so."

It's actually very calming really because it's acknowledging the reality that the senior person has a lot of judgment. That judgment is super valuable, and that's why sometimes you should overrule subordinates even when they have better ground truth. But that's your judgment. And sometimes you're, like, "I know this person, or I've worked with them for years. They have great judgment. They really disagree with me, and they have way better ground truth. I'm going to disagree and commit."

Competition

ZERO-SUM GAMES ARE unbelievably rare. Sporting events are zero-sum games. Two teams enter an arena. One's going to win; one's going to lose. Elections are zero-sum games. One candidate is going to win; one candidate is going to lose. In business, however, several competitors can do well. That's very normal. The most important thing for doing well against competition—in business and also, I think, with military adversaries—is to be both robust and nimble. And it is scale. So it's great to be in the US military because you're big. Scale is a gigantic advantage because it gives you robustness. You can take a punch. But it's also good if you can dodge a punch. And that's the nimbleness. And as you get bigger, you grow more robust.

The most important factor for nimbleness is decision-making speed. The second-most important factor is being willing to be experimental. You have to be willing to take risks. You have to be willing to fail, and people don't like failure.

I always point out that there are two different kinds of failure. There's experimental failure—that's the kind of failure you should be happy with. And there's operational failure. We've built hundreds of fulfillment centers at Amazon over the years, and we know how to do that. If we build a new fulfillment center and it's a disaster, that's just bad execution. That's not good failure. But when we are developing a new product or service or experimenting in some way, and it doesn't work, that's okay. That's great failure. And you need to distinguish between those two types of failure and really be seeking invention and innovation.

To sustain it you need the right people; you need innovative people. Innovative people will flee an organization if they can't make decisions and take risks. You might recruit them initially, but they won't stay long. Builders like to build. A lot of this stuff is very simple, really. It's just hard to do. And the other thing about competition is that you do not want to play on a level playing field. This is why you need innovation, especially in domains like space and cyber.

A level playing field is great for Monday night football. We have for decades enjoyed an unlevel playing field in areas like space and technology. I'm very nervous that this is changing rapidly. The only way to stay ahead and to keep that unlevel playing field, which is what you certainly want, is to innovate.

In the space domain we are facing adversaries who are going to innovate. So that's the real issue. If you're facing adversaries who are not good at innovating, then you don't have to be that good at innovating.

When it comes to competition, being one of the best is not good enough. Do you really want to plan for a future in which you might have to fight with somebody who is just as good as you are? I wouldn't.

Government Scrutiny
and Big Companies

ALL BIG INSTITUTIONS of any kind will and should be examined, scrutinized, and inspected. Governments should be inspected. Government institutions, big educational institutions, big nonprofits, big companies—they're going to get scrutiny. It's not personal. It's what we as a society want to have happen, and I remind people internally not to take scrutiny of Amazon personally. That will lead to a lot of wasted energy. This scrutiny is just normal. It's actually healthy and good. We want to live in a society where people are worried about big institutions.

I think we are so inventive that—whatever regulations are promulgated or however they work—they won't stop us from serving customers. Under all kinds of regulatory frameworks that I can imagine, customers are still going to want low prices. They're still going to want fast delivery. They're still going to want big selection. These are so fundamental and what we do. I would also say that it's really important that politicians and others understand the value big companies bring in and not demonize or vilify business in general or especially big companies, and for the simple reason that there are certain things that only big companies can do. I've seen this throughout Amazon's journey. I know what Amazon could do when we were ten people, and I know what we could do when we were one thousand people, and I know what we could do when we were ten thousand, and I know what we can do today when we're over half a million.

Let me give you a more vivid example. I love garage entrepreneurs and invest in a lot of their companies. I know many of them. But nobody in their garage is going to build an all-carbon-fiber, fuel-efficient Boeing 787. It's not going to happen. You need Boeing to do that. If you like your smartphone, you need Apple to do that; you need Samsung to do that. These are things that well-functioning entrepreneurial capitalism does very well. And there are market failures that no one takes care of, and you look to philanthropy and government to take care of them. So you need different models for different things. But definitely, this world would be worse off without, for example, Boeing, Apple, and Samsung.

The Climate Pledge

In September 2019, Amazon announced—and was the first signatory of—the Climate Pledge, which has the objective of meeting the goals of the Paris agreement ten years early. The remarks below were taken from the Climate Pledge's launch press conference. They include comments from Dara O'Rourke, who leads the sustainability science team at Amazon.

THOSE WHO SIGN the Climate Pledge agree to, number one, measure and report their emissions on a regular basis and, number two, to implement decarbonization strategies in line with the Paris agreement, which basically means that these are real things they are doing in their business, things they're changing in their actual business activities to eliminate carbon.

And then, third, with any remaining emissions they cannot eliminate with real change, they agree to do offsets that are credible. And what do we mean by *credible* offsets? We mean nature-based solutions.

The Climate Pledge really can only be done in collaboration with other large companies, because we're all part of each other's supply chains. So we need to work together to meet these goals. It has to be done that way. Amazon signed up to use our scale and our scope to lead the way and become a role model. It is, however, a difficult challenge for us because of our deep, large physical infrastructure. We're not only moving information around. We're also moving packages around. We deliver more than ten billion items a year, and that is physical infrastructure at real scale. So we can make the argument—and we plan to do so passionately—that if we can do this, anyone can. It's going to be challenging, but we know we can do it, and we know we have to do it.

It can only be done if there is real scientific integrity behind Amazon's every action. Dara O'Rourke explained Amazon's approach:

> Teams across all of Amazon have been working since 2016 to map and measure the company's overall environmental impacts. They have been laying the foundational layer of scientific models and data systems to build sustainability in a very Amazonian way. That is, science connected to technology connected to customer obsession to approach the scale of the sustainability challenges we all face.
>
> Over the last few years, the core of that work has been collecting data, building models, and building tools. Not just for teams to track their environmental emissions—their carbon—but to enable them to radically reduce carbon across the company and down supply chains.
>
> Amazon is a very large and complex company, and that forced us to build one of the most sophisticated carbon-accounting systems in the world. We had to build a system that could get to granular data, but at Amazon scale to give teams innovation optionality and to see the overall company view. Actionability requires this finer level of resolution of data. Our system is both comprehensive in covering the entire company and precise enough to get down to system-level optimizations.
>
> We can go all the way down to individual products, processes, and services. With Echo, for example, we need to understand

the impact of the manufacturing step back up to the data centers powering Alexa and then across to the planes, the trucks, and the packages that deliver that Echo to a customer's house.

So far, we've built five models based on an academic technique called environmental life-cycle assessment. Four are process models in transportation, in packaging, in electricity for both our fulfillment centers and data centers, and in devices. We combined internal operational data—physical data processed with financial data—with external scientific data to stitch it all together into our carbon footprint.

We're also using this data in our climate risk analysis. We have partnered with Amazon Web Services to host over 55 foundational weather, climate and sustainability datasets, leveraging the infrastructure of AWS, with cutting-edge machine-learning tools that are already being used by NGOs, academics, and governments around the world to actually solve climate problems.

We take business-specific activity data. We connect it to emissions models. We run it through an orchestration layer that stitches it all together into decision-support tools—dashboards, metrics, mechanisms that teams can use across the company to drive carbon out. Each of these models has a detailed logic and fine-grained data underneath it.

The transportation model is focused on the critical drivers of carbon, in this case vehicle types, fuel types, and routes. This allows us to analyze our existing networks and logistics and also to understand emerging technologies, emerging vehicles, alternative fuels. We're now able to model the electronic vehicles (EVs) that are coming, the drones that are coming, the next transportation innovation that will come. Ultimately this allows us to design sustainability into our future typologies, technologies, and customer innovations.

These metrics, this data, provides insights for teams across Amazon that we otherwise wouldn't have, including things that may be counterintuitive. Same-day shipping is actually our lowest carbon ship option. This is because getting inventory local to customers is almost always a sustainability win.

These systems we built—the models, the metrics—are now giving detailed views for teams across Amazon to help them reduce carbon. We are moving from totals to targeted emissions and innovations for Amazon's customers and the planet.

We want to be leaders and role models. You know, we've been in the middle of the herd on this issue, and we want to move to the forefront. We want to be leaders. We want to say to other companies that if a company of Amazon's complexity, scale, scope, and physical infrastructure can do this, so can you.

Today Amazon is at 40 percent renewable energy. We've done that by building fifteen utility-scale solar and wind farms. We've put rooftop installations on fulfillment centers and sortation centers around the world.

Where are we going? Well, on renewable energy we have committed to reaching 80 percent renewable energy by 2040. And by 2030 we're committing to being at 100 percent renewable. The team is pushing to get to 100 percent by 2025 and has a credible plan to pull that off.

We also have a lot of delivery vans, and they all burn fossil fuels today. In September 2019 we placed an order for one hundred thousand electric delivery vans to be built by a company called Rivian. A pledge like the Climate Pledge will drive the economy to start to build products and services that these large companies need to meet those commitments. This is why we invested $440 million in Rivian.

We are in partnership with the Nature Conservancy, funding something called the Right Now Climate Fund. We're contributing $100 million to reforestation. Reforestation is a great example of a nature-based solution for removing carbon from the Earth's atmosphere.

As this economy develops and people get serious about being carbon-zero through real changes to their real business activities, that is going to be a gigantic signal to the marketplace to start inventing and developing the new technologies these global companies will need to be able to meet this commitment. And so that's another reason we have to work together. We need to get a number of companies to sign up for this to really drive that market signal in a strong way. Amazon is large, but if we get lots of large companies to agree to the same thing, that will send an even stronger signal to the market—especially as the supply chains are so interconnected. Collaboration becomes the only way to do it.

The Bezos Day One Fund

The Bezos Day One Fund launched in 2018 with a $2 billion commitment to focus on making meaningful and lasting impacts in two areas: funding existing nonprofits that help families experiencing homelessness and creating a network of new, nonprofit tier-one preschools in low-income communities.

The Day 1 Families Fund issues annual leadership awards to organizations and civic groups doing compassionate, needle-moving work to provide shelter and hunger support to address the immediate needs of young families. The vision statement comes from the inspiring Mary's Place in Seattle: no child sleeps outside.

The Day 1 Academies Fund is building an organization to launch and operate a network of high-quality, full-scholarship, Montessori-inspired preschools in underserved communities. We will have the opportunity to learn, invent, and improve. And we'll use the same set of principles that have driven Amazon. Most important among those will be genuine, intense customer obsession. The customer set that this team of missionaries will serve is simple: children in underserved communities across the country.

The remarks below were made at the Economic Club of Washington on September 13, 2018, in a conversation with club president David Rubenstein.

T HE PROCESS I used to create the Day One Fund was very helpful. I solicited ideas, kind of crowdsourced them, and literally received something like forty-seven thousand responses, maybe even a little more. Some came to my inbox. Most came on social media, and I read through thousands and thousands of them. My office correlated them all and put them into buckets, and some themes emerged. A fascinating thing about crowdsourcing is just how long-tailed it is. People are interested in trying to help the world in so many different ways—all involving what you would expect. Some people are very interested in the arts and opera and think they're underfunded. A lot of people are interested in medicine and particular diseases and think that those deserve more R&D dollars. All are correct. A lot of people are very interested in homelessness, including me. A lot of people are very interested in education of all kinds, both college scholarships but also apprenticeship programs.

I'm very interested in early education, and here the apple doesn't fall far from the tree. My mother, in running the Bezos Family Foundation, has become an expert in early education. I'm a product of Montessori schools. I started at Montessori when I was two years old, and the teacher complained to my mother that was I was too task focused and that she couldn't get me to switch tasks; she would have to pick up my chair and move me. And by the way, if you ask the people who work with me, that's probably still true today.

Our schools will be free-tuition, Montessori-inspired preschool. We are going to be an operating nonprofit. I've hired an executive team. There's a leadership team. We're going to operate these schools, and we're going to put them in low-income neighborhoods. We know for a fact that a kid who falls behind has a really, really hard time catching up, and if you can give somebody a leg up when

they're two, three, or four years old, by the time they get to kinder-
garten or first grade, they're much less likely to fall behind. It can
still happen, but you've really improved their odds. Most people are
very mindful about making sure their kids get a very good preschool
education and that kind of head start. That head start builds on itself
fantastically. If you can get that starting at age two, three, four, there's
a powerful compounding effect there. So it's highly levered. That's
all that really means. The money spent there is going to pay gigantic
dividends for decades.

There will also be more traditional grantmaking philanthropy.
I'm going to hire a full-time team to identify and fund family homeless shelters.

It's Day 1. Everything I have ever done has started small. Amazon
started with a couple of people. Blue Origin started with five people
and a very, very small budget. Now the budget of Blue Origin is over
$1 billion a year. Amazon literally started with 10 people; today it is
over 750,000. That's hard to remember for others, but for me it's like
yesterday. I was driving the packages to the post office myself and
hoping one day we could afford a forklift. So for me, I've seen small
things get big, and it's part of this Day 1 mentality. I like treating
things as if they're small. Even though Amazon is a large company,
I want it to have the heart and spirit of a small one. The Day One
Fund is going to be like that. We'll wander a little bit too. We have
some very specific ideas about what we want to do, but I believe in
the power of wandering. All my best decisions in business and in life
have been made with heart, intuition, and guts, not analysis. When
you can make a decision with analysis, you should do so, but it turns
out in life that your most important decisions are always made with
instinct, intuition, taste, and heart, and that's what we'll do with this
Day One Fund too. It's part of the Day 1 mentality. As we go about
building out this network of nonprofit schools, we will learn new
things, and we'll figure out how to make it better.

The customer is going to be the child. This is so important because that is the secret sauce of Amazon. Several principles are the

foundation of Amazon, but the number-one thing by far that has made us successful is obsessive, compulsive focus on the customer as opposed to the competitor. I talk so often to other CEOs and also founders and entrepreneurs, and I can tell that even though they're talking about customers, they're really focusing on competitors. It is a huge advantage to any company if you can stay focused on your customer instead of your competitor. You have to identify who your customer is. At the *Washington Post*, for example, is the customer the people who buy advertisements from us? No. The customer is the reader, full stop. And where do advertisers want to be? Advertisers want to be where there are readers, so it's really not that complicated. Who are the customers in the school? Is it the parents? Is it the teachers? No. It is the children. We're going to be obsessively, compulsively focused on the children; we're going to be scientific when we can be, and we're going to use heart and intuition when we need to.

I intend to give away my fortune. I don't know how much of it I'm going to give away—I'm also going to invest a lot of it in Blue Origin.

I start with a mission, and if you have a mission, there are three ways to fulfill it: you can do it with government, you can do it through a nonprofit, and you can do it through a for-profit. If you can figure out how to do it with a for-profit structure, that has a lot of advantages for many reasons. One, it's self-sustaining. Take the iPhone. The last thing we need is a nonprofit company making phones. It turns out there's a healthy competitive ecosystem that likes to build these things. There's no market failure here. If, like the Gates Foundation, you look at room-temperature vaccines, there's no market for room-temperature vaccines. Anybody who can afford a vaccine can also afford a refrigerator, and so you need to start solving problems that have no market solution. And then you get to other things, like the court system and the military and so on. You can't even figure out a nonprofit model.

Where will the money go? The real answer to the question is that I'm going to give away a lot of money in a nonprofit model like the

Day One Fund. But I'm also going to invest a lot of money in something, Blue Origin, which any rational investor would say is a really bad investment, but I think it is super important. I want Blue Origin to be a thriving, self-sustaining company.

The Purpose of
Going into Space

The following remarks were made on May 9, 2019, in Washington, DC, at an event to unveil Blue Origin's lunar lander, Blue Moon.

BLUE ORIGIN IS the most important work I'm doing. I have great conviction about it, based on a simple argument: Earth is the best planet.

The big question we need to ponder is: Why do we need to go to space? My answer is different from the common "plan B" argument: the Earth gets destroyed and you want to be somewhere else. It's unmotivating and doesn't work for me. When I was in high school I wrote, "The earth is finite, and if the world economy and population are to keep expanding, space is the only way to go." I still believe this.

The question "What's the best planet in this solar system" is easy to answer because we have sent robotic probes to all the other ones. Some inspections have been flybys, but we've examined them all. Earth is the best planet—it is not close. This one is really good. My friends who want to move to Mars? I say, "Do me a favor. Go live on the top of Mount Everest for a year first and see if you like it—because it's a garden paradise compared to Mars." Don't even get me started on Venus.

Look at Earth. It is incredible. Jim Lovell, one of my real heroes, while he was circling around the moon on the Apollo 8 mission, did something amazing. He put out his thumb and realized that, with it at arm's length, he could cover the whole Earth. Everything he'd ever known, he could cover with his thumb, and he said something amazing. You know the old saying "I hope I go to heaven when I die." He said, "I realized at that moment, you go to heaven when you're born." Earth is heaven.

The astronomer Carl Sagan was so poetic: "On that blue dot, that's where everyone you know, and everyone you ever heard of, and every human being who ever lived, lived out their lives. A very small stage in a great cosmic arena." For all of human history the Earth has felt big to us, and actually in a really correct sense, it has been big. Humanity has been small. That's not true anymore. The Earth is no longer big. Humanity is big. Earth seems big to us, but it's finite. We have to realize that there are immediate problems, things that we need to work on, and we are working on those things. They're urgent. I'm talking about poverty, hunger, homelessness, pollution, overfishing in the oceans. The list of immediate problems is very long, and we need to work on those things urgently, in the here and now. But there are also long-range problems: we need to work on them too, and they take a long time to solve. You can't wait until the long-range problems are urgent to work on them. We can do both. We can work on the problems in the here and now, and we can get started on the long-range problems.

We want to go to space to protect this planet. That's why the company is named Blue Origin—for the blue planet, which is where we're from. But we don't want to face a civilization of stasis, and that is the real issue if we just stay on this planet—that's the long-term issue.

A very fundamental long-range problem is that we will run out of energy on Earth. This is just arithmetic. It's going to happen. As animals, humans use ninety-seven watts of power—that's our metabolic rate as animals—but as members of the developed world, we use ten thousand watts of power. And we get a lot of benefit from it. We live in an era of dynamism and growth. You live a better life than your grandparents did, and your grandparents lived better lives than their grandparents did, and a big part of that is the abundance of energy we have been able to harvest and use to our benefit. There are many good things that happen when we use energy. When you go to the hospital, you're using a lot of energy. Medical equipment, transportation, the kinds of entertainments that we enjoy, the medications we use—all these things require a tremendous amount of energy. We don't want to stop using energy. But our use levels are unsustainable.

The historic compounding rate of global energy usage is 3 percent a year. It doesn't sound like very much, but over many years the compounding becomes extreme. Three percent compounded annually is the equivalent of doubling human energy use every twenty-five years. If you take global energy use today, you can power everything by covering Nevada in solar cells. Now, that seems challenging, but it also seems possible, and it is mostly desert anyway. But in just a couple hundred years, at that 3 percent historic compounding rate, we'll need to cover the entire surface of the Earth in solar cells. Now, that's not going to happen. That's a very impractical solution, and we can be sure it won't work. So what can we do?

Well, one thing we can do is focus on efficiency, and that is a good idea. The problem, though, is that it's already assumed. As we've been growing our energy usage 3 percent a year for centuries, we have always focused on efficiency. Let me give you some examples. Two hundred years ago you had to work eighty-four hours to afford one hour of artificial light. Today you have to work 1.5 seconds to afford an hour of artificial light. We've moved from candles to oil lamps to incandescent bulbs to LEDs and gotten tremendous efficiency gains. Another example is air transportation. In the half century of commercial aviation, we've seen a fourfold efficiency gain. Half a century ago it took 109 gallons of fuel to fly one person across the country. Today, in a modern 787, it takes only 24. It's an incredible improvement. It's very dramatic.

How about computation? Computational efficiency has increased one trillion times. The Univac could do fifteen calculations with one kilowatt second of energy. A modern processor can do seventeen trillion calculations with one kilowatt second of energy. Now, what happens when we get very efficient? We use more of these things. Artificial light has gotten very inexpensive, so we use a lot of it. Air transport has gotten very inexpensive, so we use a lot of it. Computation has gotten very inexpensive, so we even have SnapChat.

We have an ever-increasing demand for energy. And even in the face of increasing efficiency, we will be using more and more energy. That 3 percent compound growth rate already assumes great efficiency gains in the future. What happens when unlimited demand meets finite resources? The answer is incredibly simple: rationing. That's the path we would find ourselves on, and that path would lead, for the first time, to your grandchildren and their grandchildren having worse lives than you. That's a bad path.

There's good news: if we move out into the solar system, we will have, for all practical purposes, unlimited resources. So we get to choose: Do we want stasis and rationing? Or do we want dynamism and growth? This is an easy choice. We know what we want. We just need to get busy. We could have a trillion humans in the solar system, which means we'd have a thousand Mozarts and a thousand Einsteins. This would be an incredible civilization.

What could this future look like? Where would a trillion humans live? Gerard O'Neill, a professor of physics at Princeton University, looked at this question very carefully, and he asked a very precise question that no one had ever asked before: "Is a planetary surface the best place for humans to expand into the solar system?" He and his students set to work on answering that question, and they came to a very surprising, for them, counterintuitive answer: no.

Why not? Well, they came up with a bunch of problems. One is that other planetary surfaces aren't that big. You're talking about maybe a doubling at best, which is not that much. And they're a long way away. Round-trip times to Mars are on the order of years, and launch opportunities to Mars occur only once every twenty-six months, which is a very significant logistics problem. And finally, you're far enough away so that you're not going to be able to do real-time communications with Earth. You're going to be limited by a speed-of-light lag.

Most fundamentally, these other planetary surfaces do not and cannot have Earth-normal gravity. You're going to be stuck with whatever gravitational field they have. In the case of Mars, that's one-third G. So, instead, O'Neill and his students came up with the idea of manufactured worlds, rotated to create artificial gravity with centrifugal force. These are very large structures, miles on end, and they hold a million people or more each.

A space colony would be very different from the International Space Station. Inside it would have high-speed transport, agricultural areas, cities. The stations don't all have to have the same gravity. You could have a recreational colony that kept zero G so you could go flying with your own wings. Some would be national parks. These would be really pleasant places to live. Some of these O'Neill colonies might choose to replicate Earth cities. They might pick historical cities and mimic them in some way. There would be whole new kinds of architecture. These are ideal climates. This is Maui on its best day all year long—no rain, no storms, no earthquakes.

What does the architecture even look like when it no longer has the primary purpose of shelter? We'll find out. But these colonies will be beautiful—people are going to want to live there—and they can be close to Earth so that you can return, which is important because people are going to want to return to Earth. They're not going to want to leave Earth forever. They'll also be really easy to travel between. Going between these O'Neill colonies, from one to another—to visit friends, to visit family, to visit one that's a recreational area—would require very, very low amounts of energy for quick transportation. It would be a day trip.

Professor O'Neill once appeared on television with the famous science-fiction author Isaac Asimov. The host asked Asimov a very good question: "Did anybody in science fiction ever predict [O'Neill colonies,] and if not, why not?" Asimov had a very good answer: "Nobody did, really, because we've all been planet chauvinists. We've all believed people should live on the surface of a planet, of a world. In my writing I've had colonies on the moon. So have a hundred other science fiction writers. The closest I came to a manufactured world in free space was to suggest that we go out to the asteroid belt and hollow out the asteroids and make ships out of them. It never occurred to me to bring the material from the asteroids in towards the earth where conditions are pleasanter and build the worlds there."

Planetary chauvinists! Where will building this vision, these O'Neill colonies, take us? What will it mean for Earth? Earth will end up zoned residential and light industry. It'll be a beautiful place to live. It'll be a beautiful place to visit. It'll be a beautiful place to go to college and to do some light industry. But heavy industry and all the polluting industry—all the things that are damaging our planet—will be done off Earth.

We would thereby preserve this unique gem of a planet, which is completely irreplaceable. There is no plan B. We need to save our Earth, and we shouldn't give up on a future of dynamism and growth for our grandchildren's grandchildren. We can have both.

Who is going to do this work? Not me. This is a big vision that will take a long time to realize. Kids in school today and their children will do it. They will build whole industries with thousands of future companies encompassing whole ecosystems. There will be entrepreneurial activity, unleashing creative people to come up with new ideas about how to use space. But those entrepreneurial companies cannot exist today. It's impossible because the price of admission to do interesting things in space right now is just too high. Because there's no infrastructure.

I started Amazon in 1994. All of the heavy-lifting infrastructure needed for Amazon to exist was already in place. We did not have to build a transportation system to deliver packages. It existed already. If we'd had to build that, we would have needed billions of dollars in capital. But it was there. It was called the US Postal Service, Deutsche Post, the Royal Mail, UPS, and FedEx. We got to stand on top of that infrastructure. The same was true of payment systems. Did we have to invent a payment system and roll that out? That would have taken billions of dollars and many decades. But no, it already existed. It was called the credit card. Did we have to invent computers? No, they were already in most homes, mostly to play games, but they were there. That infrastructure already existed. Did we have to build a telecom network, requiring billions more dollars? No, we didn't. It was in place, mostly to make long-distance phone calls and built by global telecom carriers like AT&T and their equivalents around the world. Infrastructure lets entrepreneurs do amazing things.

Those O'Neill colonies will be built by today's kids and their children and grandchildren. The job of building the infrastructure so these colonies can be created will start with my generation. We're going to build a road to space, and then amazing things will happen. Then you'll see entrepreneurial creativity. Then you'll have space entrepreneurs start a company in their dorm room. That can't happen today.

So how are we really going to build O'Neill colonies? Nobody knows. I don't know. Future generations will figure out the details. But we do know that there are certain gates to pass through, certain prerequisites to meet. If we don't do these, we will never get there, and it's really nice to know what those things are because you can work on them, with great confidence that they're going to be useful. However the details of that future vision evolve, two things will be essential. First, we must have a radical reduction in launch cost. Launches are simply too expensive today. And second, we have to use in-space resources. Earth has a very powerful gravitational field, and lifting all of our resources off of Earth just isn't going to work. We need to be able to use resources that are already in space.

Named after Mercury astronaut Alan Shepard, the first American to go to space, *New Shepard* is Blue Origin's reusable suborbital rocket system designed to take astronauts and research payloads past the Kármán line, the internationally recognized boundary of space. *New Glenn*, named for astronaut John Glenn, is a single-configuration, heavy-lift launch vehicle capable of carrying people and payloads routinely into Earth orbit and beyond.

One thing I'm very excited about with *New Shepard* is using it to get a lot of practice. The most-flown vehicles may fly a couple of dozen times a year, launching payloads into orbit. You never get really good when you do something just a couple of dozen times a year.

Let's say you're going to have some surgery. You should make sure the surgeon does that operation at least five times a week. Real data backs up the fact that a surgery is much safer if your surgeon is practicing it at least five times a week. And so we need to be going to space very frequently in a very routine way. One reason aviation is so safe today is because we do have so much practice.

We need to have more missions. If your payloads cost hundreds of millions of dollars, they actually cost more than the launch. This puts a lot of pressure on the launch vehicle not to change, to be very stable—reliability becomes much more important than cost. This actually drives you in the wrong direction of having fewer launches and very expensive satellites, and that's what you see happening in many cases.

At Blue Origin we want to try to get on that practice groove, and to do that we have to have an operable, reusable vehicle. The key point here is operability. The space shuttle was only reusable in the most daunting of senses. In reality, NASA would bring the space shuttle back, inspect it in very elaborate ways, and then refly it. It would've been better to have an expendable vehicle. You can't fly your 767 airplane to its destination and then x-ray the whole thing, disassemble it all, and expect to have acceptable costs. And so reusability vis-à-vis the airplane, versus the air shuttle, is really the key. Our goal is to drive down costs using reusability, and the vision is to figure out how there can really be dynamic entrepreneurialism in space.

I'm incredibly proud of the amazing progress the Blue Origin team has made on reusable launch vehicles with *New Shepard*. We have had eleven consecutive landings. We've used two boosters. One has flown five times consecutively, and the other has flown six times consecutively. There has been almost no refurbishment between flights. That's how you reduce launch cost. You need to have reusable vehicles. Until now we have been using launch vehicles one time and throwing them away. You also can't have fake reusability, where you bring the vehicle back and then do a lot of refurbishment, which is also very expensive. It's incredibly exciting that we're going to be flying humans on *New Shepard* soon.

When we built *New Shepard*, a suborbital vehicle designed for space tourism, we made some very curious technology decisions. It is, first of all, powered by liquid hydrogen, the highest-performing rocket fuel but also the most difficult to work with. It's not needed for a suborbital mission, but we chose it because we knew we were going to need it for the next stage. We wanted to get practice with that hardest-to-use but highest-performing propellant. We made the same decision with vertical landing for *New Shepard*, even though other landing mechanisms would have worked at this scale. The great thing about vertical landing is it scales up really well. It's very counterintuitive, but the bigger the vehicle, the easier vertical landing gets. Vertical landing is like balancing a broom on your fingertip. You can balance a broom, but try balancing a pencil. The moment of inertia of the pencil is too small. Right from the start, we wanted to build a human-rated system so we would be forced to think clearly about safety and reliability, escape systems—all the things we knew we would need to have practice with in order to build our next generation of vehicle. So it's all about practice.

New Glenn is *New Shepard*'s big brother, big enough that *New Shepard* will fit in the payload bay of *New Glenn*. It's a very large vehicle, with 3.9 million pounds of thrust. I get asked a very interesting question from time to time: "Jeff, what's going to change over the next ten years?" And I enjoy playing with the answer. That's a fun dinner conversation. But there's an even more important question I almost never get asked: "What's not going to change over the next ten years?" And that question is so important because you can build your plans around those things. So I know for a fact that Amazon customers are going to want low prices ten years from now. That's not going to change. Customers are going to want fast delivery. They're going to want big selection. So all the energy we've put into those things will continue to pay dividends. It is impossible to imagine a customer coming to me ten years from now and saying, "Jeff, I love Amazon. I just wish you delivered a little more slowly" or "I just wish the prices were a little higher." That's not going to happen. When you can figure out the things that are going to remain true under almost all circumstances, then you can put energy into them. We know what those things are for *New Glenn*. It's cost, reliability, and on-time launches. Each one needs improvement before we can enter the next phase of really going out into the solar system, and I know these things are stable in time. We are not going to have a *New Glenn* customer come to us in ten years and say, "Jeff, I wish the rocket just, you know, failed a little more often" or "I wish it was more expensive or that you were late on my launch dates." By the way, availability and launching on time are really big problems underappreciated by most people who aren't directly in the space industry. Delays really snarl things up and cost the payload customers a lot of money. So these things won't change. We're going to put energy into them. The whole vehicle is designed around those three things.

Reusability is absolutely the key to radically reducing launch costs. People sometimes wonder how expensive the fuel is and whether the fuel is a problem. Liquefied natural gas is very inexpensive. Even though there are millions of pounds of propellant on *New Glenn,* the cost of fuel and oxidizer is less than $1 million—insignificant in the scheme of things. The need to throw hardware away is the reason why launching into orbit is so expensive today. It's like driving your car to the mall and then throwing it away after one trip. That's going to make trips to the mall very expensive.

The second gate we must go through is in-space resources. We have to use them, and we have a gift: this nearby body called the moon. We know a lot now about the moon that we didn't know back in the Apollo days or even just twenty years ago. One of the most important things we know is that there's water, an incredibly valuable resource, on the moon in the form of ice. It's in the permanently shadowed craters on the poles of the moon. You can use electrolysis to break down water into hydrogen and oxygen, and you have propellants. Another great thing about the moon, another reason it's a gift, is that it is nearby, just three days away. And you don't have the same launch constraints, like the twenty-six months between launches that we have with Mars. You can go to the moon just about any time you want. And, of great importance for building large objects in space, the moon has six times less gravity than Earth. When you get resources from the moon, you can get them into free space at very low cost. It takes twenty-four times less energy to lift a pound off the moon than it does off the Earth. That is a huge lever.

But the moon also needs infrastructure. One way to build infrastructure will be through vehicles such as *Blue Moon,* a very large lander we have been working on for several years that soft-lands in a precise way, 3.6 metric tons onto the lunar surface. The stretched-tank variant of it will soft-land 6.5 metric tons onto the lunar surface. The deck is designed to be a very simple interface so that a great variety of payloads can be placed onto the top deck and secured.

Jeff Bezos reveals the *Blue Moon* Lunar Lander, May 9, 2019
(© Blue Origin)

With its davits system, inspired by naval systems, things are lowered off the deck onto the surface of the moon. And the davits can be customized for the particular payloads.

There's a lot of interesting science to be done on the moon, especially on the poles, and Blue Origin has formed a Science Advisory Board to make sure the science gets done right and we get the most bang for our buck. We also have customers for *Blue Moon,* and they are going to be deploying science missions to the moon as well. People are very excited about this capability to soft-land their cargo, rovers, and science experiments onto the surface of the moon in a precise way. There is no capability to do that today.

Vice President Mike Pence said that it's the stated policy of the Donald J. Trump administration and the United States to return American astronauts to the moon within the next five years. I love this. It's the right thing to do, and for those of you doing the arithmetic at home, that's 2024. And we can help meet that timeline. It's time to go back to the moon, this time to stay.

It's Still Day One
for America

Thank you, Chairman Cicilline, Ranking Member Sensenbrenner, and members of the Subcommittee. I'm Jeff Bezos. I founded Amazon twenty-six years ago with the long-term mission of making it Earth's most customer-centric company.

My mom, Jackie, had me when she was a seventeen-year-old high school student in Albuquerque, New Mexico. Being pregnant in high school was not popular in Albuquerque in 1964. It was difficult for her. When they tried to kick her out of school, my grandfather went to bat for her. After some negotiation, the principal said, "OK, she can stay and finish high school, but she can't do any extracurricular activities, and she can't have a locker." My grandfather took the deal, and my mother finished high school, though she wasn't allowed to walk across the stage with her classmates to get her diploma. Determined to keep up with her education, she enrolled in night school, picking classes led by professors who would let her bring an infant to class. She would show up with two duffel bags—one full of textbooks, and one packed with diapers, bottles, and anything that would keep me interested and quiet for a few minutes.

My dad's name is Miguel. He adopted me when I was four years old. He was sixteen when he came to the United States from Cuba as part of Operation Pedro Pan, shortly after Castro took over. My dad arrived in America alone. His parents felt he'd be safer here. His mom imagined America would be cold, so she made him a jacket sewn entirely out of cleaning cloths, the only material they had on hand. We still have that jacket; it hangs in my parents' dining room. My dad spent two weeks at Camp Matecumbe, a refugee center in Florida, before being moved to a Catholic mission in Wilmington, Delaware. He was lucky to get to the mission, but even so, he didn't speak English and didn't have an easy path. What he did have was a lot of grit and determination. He received a scholarship to college in Albuquerque, which is where he met my mom. You get different gifts in life, and one of my great gifts is my mom and dad. They have been incredible role models for me and my siblings our entire lives.

YOU LEARN DIFFERENT THINGS from your grandparents than you do from your parents, and I had the opportunity to spend my summers from ages four to sixteen on my grandparents' ranch in Texas. My grandfather was a civil servant and a rancher—he worked on space technology and missile-defense systems in the 1950s and 1960s for the Atomic Energy Commission—and he was self-reliant and resourceful. When you're in the middle of nowhere, you don't pick up a phone and call somebody when something breaks. You fix it yourself. As a kid, I got to see him solve many seemingly unsolvable problems himself, whether he was restoring a broken-down Caterpillar bulldozer or doing his own veterinary work. He taught me that you can take on hard problems. When you have a setback, you get back up and try again. You can invent your way to a better place.

I took these lessons to heart as a teenager, and became a garage inventor. I invented an automatic gate closer out of cement-filled tires, a solar cooker out of an umbrella and tinfoil, and alarms made from baking pans to entrap my siblings.

The concept for Amazon came to me in 1994. The idea of building an online bookstore with millions of titles—something that simply couldn't exist in the physical world—was exciting to me. At the time, I was working at an investment firm in New York City. When I told my boss I was leaving, he took me on a long walk in Central Park. After a lot of listening, he finally said, "You know what, Jeff, I think this is a good idea, but it would be a better idea for somebody who didn't already have a good job." He convinced me to think about it for two days before making a final decision. It was a decision I made with my heart and not my head. When I'm eighty and reflecting back, I want to have minimized the number of regrets that I have in my life. And most of our regrets are acts of omission—the things we didn't try, the paths untraveled. Those are the things that haunt us. And I decided that if I didn't at least give it my best shot, I was going to regret not trying to participate in this thing called the internet that I thought was going to be a big deal.

The initial start-up capital for Amazon.com came primarily from my parents, who invested a large fraction of their life savings in something they didn't understand. They weren't making a bet on Amazon or the concept of a bookstore on the internet. They were making a bet on their son. I told them that I thought there was a 70 percent chance they would lose their investment, and they did it anyway. It took more than fifty meetings for me to raise $1 million from investors, and over the course of all those meetings, the most common question was, "What's the internet?"

Unlike many other countries around the world, this great nation we live in supports and does not stigmatize entrepreneurial risk-taking. I walked away from a steady job into a Seattle garage to found my startup, fully understanding that it might not work. It feels like just yesterday I was driving the packages to the post office myself, dreaming that one day we might be able to afford a forklift.

Amazon's success was anything but preordained. Investing in Amazon early on was a very risky proposition. From our founding through the end of 2001, our business had cumulative losses of nearly $3 billion, and we did not have a profitable quarter until the fourth quarter of that year. Smart analysts predicted Barnes & Noble would steamroll us, and branded us "Amazon.toast." In 1999, after we'd been in business for nearly five years, Barron's headlined a story about our impending demise "Amazon.bomb." My annual shareholder letter for 2000 started with a one-word sentence: "Ouch." At the pinnacle of the internet bubble our stock price peaked at $116, and then after the bubble burst our stock went down to $6. Experts and pundits thought we were going out of business. It took a lot of smart people with a willingness to take a risk with me, and a willingness to stick to our convictions, for Amazon to survive and ultimately to succeed.

And it wasn't just those early years. In addition to good luck and great people, we have been able to succeed as a company only because we have continued to take big risks. To invent you have to experiment, and if you know in advance that it's going to work, it's not an experiment. Outsized returns come from betting against conventional wisdom, but conventional wisdom is usually right. A lot of observers characterized Amazon Web Services as a risky distraction when we started. "What does selling compute and storage have to do with selling books?" they wondered. No one asked for AWS. It turned out the world was ready and hungry for cloud computing but didn't know it yet. We were right about AWS, but the truth is we've also taken plenty of risks that didn't pan out. In fact, Amazon has made billions of dollars of failures. Failure inevitably comes along with invention and risk-taking, which is why we try to make Amazon the best place in the world to fail.

Since our founding, we have strived to maintain a "Day One" mentality at the company. By that I mean approaching everything we do with the energy and entrepreneurial spirit of Day One. Even though Amazon is a large company, I have always believed that if we commit ourselves to maintaining a Day One mentality as a critical part of our DNA, we can have both the scope and capabilities of a large company and the spirit and heart of a small one.

In my view, obsessive customer focus is by far the best way to achieve and maintain Day One vitality. Why? Because customers are always beautifully, wonderfully dissatisfied, even when they report being happy and business is great. Even when they don't yet know it, customers want something better, and a constant desire to delight customers drives us to constantly invent on their behalf. As a result, by focusing obsessively on customers, we are internally driven to improve our services, add benefits and features, invent new products, lower prices, and speed up shipping times—*before* we have to. No customer ever asked Amazon to create the Prime membership program, but it sure turns out they wanted it. And I could give you many such examples. Not every business takes this customer-first approach, but we do, and it's our greatest strength.

Customer trust is hard to win and easy to lose. When you let customers make your business what it is, then they will be loyal to you—right up to the second that someone else offers them better service. We know that customers are perceptive and smart. We take as an article of faith that customers will notice when we work hard to do the right thing, and that by doing so again and again, we will earn trust. You earn trust slowly, over time, by doing hard things well—delivering on time; offering everyday low prices; making promises and keeping them; making principled decisions, even when they're unpopular; and giving customers more time to spend with their families by inventing more convenient ways of shopping, reading, and automating their homes. As I have said since my first shareholder letter in 1997, we make decisions based on the long-term value we create as we invent to meet customer needs. When we're criticized for those choices, we listen and look at ourselves in the mirror. When we think our critics are right, we change. When we make mistakes, we apologize. But when you look in the mirror, assess the criticism, and still believe you're doing the right thing, no force in the world should be able to move you.

Fortunately, our approach is working. Eighty percent of Americans have a favorable impression of Amazon overall, according to leading independent polls. Who do Americans trust more than Amazon "to do the right thing?" Only their primary physicians and the military, according to a January 2020 Morning Consult survey. Researchers at Georgetown and New York University found in 2018 that Amazon trailed only the military among all respondents to a survey on institutional and brand trust. Among Republicans, we trailed only the military and local police; among Democrats, we were at the top, leading every branch of government, universities, and the press. In Fortune's 2020 rankings of the World's Most Admired Companies, we came in second place (Apple was #1). We are grateful that customers notice the hard work we do on their behalf, and that they reward us with their trust. Working to earn and keep that trust is the single biggest driver of Amazon's Day One culture.

The company most of you know as Amazon is the one that sends you your online orders in the brown boxes with the smile on the side. That's where we started, and retail remains our largest business by far, accounting for over 80 percent of our total revenue. The very nature of that business is getting products to customers. Those operations need to be close to customers, and we can't outsource these jobs to China or anywhere else. To fulfill our promises to customers in this country, we need American workers to get products to American customers. When customers shop on Amazon, they are helping to create jobs in their local communities. As a result, Amazon directly employs a million people, many of them entry-level and paid by the hour. We don't just employ highly educated computer scientists and MBAs in Seattle and Silicon Valley. We hire and train hundreds of thousands of people in states across the country such as West Virginia, Tennessee, Kansas, and Idaho. These employees are package stowers, mechanics, and plant managers. For many, it's their first job. For some, these jobs are a stepping-stone to other careers, and we are proud to help them with that. We are spending more than $700 million to give more than 100,000 Amazon employees access to training programs in fields such as healthcare, transportation, machine learning, and cloud computing. That program is called Career Choice, and we pay 95 percent of tuition and fees toward a certificate or diploma for in-demand, high-paying fields, regardless of whether it's relevant to a career at Amazon.

Patricia Soto, one of our associates, is a Career Choice success story. Patricia always wanted to pursue a career in the medical field to help care for others, but with only a high school diploma and facing the costs of post-secondary education, she wasn't sure she'd be able to accomplish that goal. After earning her medical certification through Career Choice, Patricia left Amazon to start her new career as a medical assistant at Sutter Gould Medical Foundation, supporting a pulmonary medicine doctor. Career Choice has given Patricia and so many others a shot at a second career that once seemed out of reach.

Amazon has invested more than $270 billion in the US over the last decade. Beyond our own workforce, Amazon's investments have created nearly 700,000 indirect jobs in fields like construction, building services, and hospitality. Our hiring and investments have brought much-needed jobs and added hundreds of millions of dollars in economic activity to areas like Fall River, Massachusetts, California's Inland Empire, and Rust Belt states like Ohio. During the COVID-19 crisis, we hired an additional 175,000 employees, including many laid off from other jobs during the economic shutdown. We spent more than $4 billion in the second quarter alone to get essential products to customers and keep our employees safe during the COVID-19 crisis. And a dedicated team of Amazon employees from across the company has created a program to regularly test our workers for COVID-19. We look forward to sharing our learnings with other interested companies and government partners.

The global retail market we compete in is strikingly large and extraordinarily competitive. Amazon accounts for less than 1 percent of the $25 trillion global retail market and less than 4 percent of retail in the US. Unlike industries that are winner-take-all, there's room in retail for many winners. For example, more than eighty retailers in the US alone earn over $1 billion in annual revenue. Like any retailer, we know that the success of our store depends entirely on customers' satisfaction with their experience in our store. Every day, Amazon competes against large, established players like Target, Costco, Kroger, and, of course, Walmart—a company more than twice Amazon's size. And while we have always focused on producing a great customer experience for retail sales done primarily online, sales initiated online are now an even larger growth area for other stores. Walmart's online sales grew 74 percent in the first quarter. And customers are increasingly flocking to services invented by other stores that Amazon still can't match at the scale of other large companies, like curbside pickup and in-store returns. The COVID-19 pandemic has put a spotlight on these trends, which have been growing for years. In recent months, curbside pickup of online orders has increased over 200 percent in part due to COVID-19 concerns. We also face new competition from the likes of Shopify and Instacart—companies that enable traditionally physical stores to put up a full online store almost instantaneously and to deliver products directly to customers in new and innovative ways—and a growing list of omnichannel business models. Like almost every other segment of our economy, technology is used everywhere in retail and has only made retail more competitive, whether online, in physical stores, or in the various combinations of the two that make up most stores today. And we and all other stores are acutely aware that, regardless of how the best features of "online" and "physical" stores are combined, we are all competing for and serving the same customers. The range of retail competitors and related services is constantly changing, and the only real constant in retail is customers' desire for lower prices, better selection, and convenience.

It's also important to understand that Amazon's success depends overwhelmingly on the success of the thousands of small and medium-sized businesses that also sell their products in Amazon's stores. Back in 1999, we took what at the time was the unprecedented step of welcoming third-party sellers into our stores and enabling them to offer their products right alongside our own. Internally, this was extremely controversial, with many disagreeing and some predicting this would be the beginning of a long, losing battle. We didn't have to invite third-party sellers into the store. We could have kept this valuable real estate for ourselves. But we committed to the idea that over the long term it would increase selection for customers, and that more satisfied customers would be great for both third-party sellers and for Amazon. And that's what happened. Within a year of adding those sellers, third-party sales accounted for 5 percent of unit sales, and it quickly became clear that customers loved the convenience of being able to shop for the best products and to see prices from different sellers all in the same store. These small and medium-sized third-party businesses now add significantly more product selection to Amazon's stores than Amazon's own retail operation. Third-party sales now account for approximately 60 percent of physical product sales on Amazon, and those sales are growing faster than Amazon's own retail sales. We guessed that it wasn't a zero-sum game. And we were right—the whole pie did grow, third-party sellers did very well and are growing fast, and that has been great for customers and for Amazon.

There are now 1.7 million small and medium-sized businesses around the world selling in Amazon's stores. More than 200,000 entrepreneurs worldwide surpassed $100,000 in sales in our stores in 2019. On top of that, we estimate that third-party businesses selling in Amazon's stores have created over 2.2 million new jobs around the world.

One of those sellers is Sherri Yukel, who wanted to change careers to be home more for her children. She started handcrafting gifts and party supplies for friends as a hobby, and eventually began selling her products on Amazon. Today, Sherri's company employs nearly eighty people and has a global customer base. Another is Christine Krogue, a stay-at-home mother of five in Salt Lake City. Christine started a business selling baby clothes through her own website before taking a chance on Amazon. She has since seen her sales more than double, and she's been able to expand her product line and hire a team of part-time employees. Selling on Amazon has allowed Sherri and Christine to grow their own businesses and satisfy customers on their own terms.

And it is striking to remember how recent all of this is. We did not start out as the largest marketplace—eBay was many times our size. It was only by focusing on supporting sellers and giving them the best tools we could invent that we were able to succeed and eventually surpass eBay. One such tool is Fulfillment by Amazon, which enables our third-party sellers to stow their inventory in our fulfillment centers, and we take on all logistics, customer service, and product returns. By dramatically simplifying all of those challenging aspects of the selling experience in a cost-effective way, we have helped many thousands of sellers grow their businesses on Amazon. Our success may help explain the wide proliferation of marketplaces of all types and sizes around the world. This includes US companies like Walmart, eBay, Etsy, and Target, as well as retailers based overseas but selling globally, such as Alibaba and Rakuten. These marketplaces further intensify competition within retail.

The trust customers put in us every day has allowed Amazon to create more jobs in the United States over the past decade than any other company—hundreds of thousands of jobs across 42 states. Amazon employees make a minimum of $15 an hour, more than double the federal minimum wage (which we have urged Congress to increase). We've challenged other large retailers to match our $15 minimum wage. Target did so recently, and just last week so did Best Buy. We welcome them, and they remain the only ones to have done so. We do not skimp on benefits, either. Our full-time hourly employees receive the same benefits as our salaried headquarters employees, including comprehensive health insurance starting on the first day of employment, a 401(k) retirement plan, and parental leave, including 20 weeks of paid maternity leave. I encourage you to benchmark our pay and benefits against any of our retail competitors.

More than 80 percent of Amazon shares are owned by outsiders, and over the last twenty-six years—starting from zero—we've created more than $1 trillion of wealth for those outside shareholders. Who are those shareowners? They are pension funds: fire, police, and school teacher pension funds. Others are 401(k)s—mutual funds that own pieces of Amazon. University endowments, too, and the list goes on. Many people will retire better because of the wealth we've created for so many, and we're enormously proud of this.

At Amazon, customer obsession has made us what we are, and allowed us to do ever greater things. I know what Amazon could do when we were 10 people. I know what we could do when we were 1,000 people, and when we were 10,000 people. And I know what we can do today when we're nearly a million. I love garage entrepreneurs—I was one. But, just like the world needs small companies, it also needs large ones. There are things small companies simply can't do. I don't care how good an entrepreneur you are, you're not going to build an all-fiber Boeing 787 in your garage.

Our scale allows us to make a meaningful impact on important societal issues. The Climate Pledge is a commitment made by Amazon and joined by other companies to meet the goals of the Paris Agreement ten years early and be net-zero carbon by 2040. We plan to meet the pledge, in part, by purchasing 100,000 electric delivery vans from Rivian—a Michigan-based producer of electric vehicles. Amazon aims to have 10,000 of Rivian's new electric vans on the road as early as 2022, and all 100,000 vehicles on the road by 2030. Globally, Amazon operates ninety-one solar and wind projects that have the capacity to generate over 2,900 MW and deliver more than 7.6 million MWh of energy annually—enough to power more than 680,000 US homes. Amazon is also investing $100 million in global reforestation projects through the Right Now Climate Fund, including $10 million Amazon committed in April to conserve, restore, and support sustainable forestry, wildlife, and nature-based solutions across the Appalachian Mountains—funding two innovative projects in collaboration with The Nature Conservancy. Four global companies—Verizon, Reckitt Benckiser, Infosys, and Oak View Group—recently signed The Climate Pledge, and we continue to encourage others to join us in this fight. Together, we will use our size and scale to address the climate crisis right away. And last month, Amazon introduced The Climate Pledge Fund, started with $2 billion in funding from Amazon. The Fund will support the development of sustainable technologies and services that in turn will enable Amazon and other companies to meet The Climate Pledge. The Fund will invest in visionary entrepreneurs and innovators who are building products and services to help companies reduce their carbon impact and operate more sustainably.

We recently opened the largest homeless shelter in Washington state—and it's located inside one of our newest headquarters buildings in downtown Seattle. The shelter is for Mary's Place, an incredible Seattle-based nonprofit. The shelter, part of Amazon's $100 million investment in Mary's Place, spans eight floors and can accommodate up to 200 family members each night. It has its own health clinic and provides critical tools and services to help families fighting homelessness get back on their feet. And there is dedicated space for Amazon to provide weekly pro-bono legal clinics offering counsel on credit and debt issues, personal injury, housing and tenant rights. Since 2018, Amazon's legal team has supported hundreds of Mary's Place guests and volunteered more than 1,000 pro-bono hours.

Amazon Future Engineer is a global childhood-to-career program designed to inspire, educate, and prepare thousands of children and young adults from underrepresented and underserved communities to pursue a computer science career. The program funds computer science coursework and professional teacher development for hundreds of elementary schools, introductory and AP Computer Science classes for more than 2,000 schools in underserved communities across the country, and 100 four-year, $40,000 college scholarships to computer science students from low-income backgrounds. Those scholarship recipients also receive guaranteed internships at Amazon. There is a diversity pipeline problem in tech, and this has an outsized impact on the Black community. We want to invest in building out the next generation of technical talent for the industry and expanding the opportunities for underrepresented minorities. We also want to accelerate this change right now. To find the best talent for technical and non-technical roles, we actively partner with historically Black colleges and universities on our recruiting, internship, and upskilling initiatives.

Let me close by saying that I believe Amazon should be scrutinized. We should scrutinize all large institutions, whether they're companies, government agencies, or non-profits. Our responsibility is to make sure we pass such scrutiny with flying colors.

It's not a coincidence that Amazon was born in this country. More than any other place on Earth, new companies can start, grow, and thrive here in the US. Our country embraces resourcefulness and self-reliance, and it embraces builders who start from scratch. We nurture entrepreneurs and start-ups with stable rule of law, the finest university system in the world, the freedom of democracy, and a deeply accepted culture of risk-taking. Of course, this great nation of ours is far from perfect. Even as we remember Congressman John Lewis and honor his legacy, we're in the middle of a much-needed race reckoning. We also face the challenges of climate change and income inequality, and we're stumbling through the crisis of a global pandemic. Still, the rest of the world would love even the tiniest sip of the elixir we have here in the US. Immigrants like my dad see what a treasure this country is—they have perspective and can often see it even more clearly than those of us who were lucky enough to

 Jeff Bezos founded Amazon.com in 1994 with the mission to be Earth's most customer-centric company. Jeff is also the founder of aerospace company Blue Origin and is owner of the *Washington Post*. In 2018 he founded the Bezos Day One Fund, which focuses on funding nonprofits that help homeless families, and on creating a network of preschools in low-income communities. Jeff graduated summa cum laude, Phi Beta Kappa, in electrical engineering and computer science from Princeton University in 1986 and was named *TIME* magazine's Person of the Year in 1999.

PublicAffairs is a publishing house founded in 1997. It is a tribute to the standards, values, and flair of three persons who have served as mentors to countless reporters, writers, editors, and book people of all kinds, including me.

I. F. STONE, proprietor of *I. F. Stone's Weekly*, combined a commitment to the First Amendment with entrepreneurial zeal and reporting skill and became one of the great independent journalists in American history. At the age of eighty, Izzy published *The Trial of Socrates*, which was a national bestseller. He wrote the book after he taught himself ancient Greek.

BENJAMIN C. BRADLEE was for nearly thirty years the charismatic editorial leader of *The Washington Post*. It was Ben who gave the *Post* the range and courage to pursue such historic issues as Watergate. He supported his reporters with a tenacity that made them fearless and it is no accident that so many became authors of influential, best-selling books.

ROBERT L. BERNSTEIN, the chief executive of Random House for more than a quarter century, guided one of the nation's premier publishing houses. Bob was personally responsible for many books of political dissent and argument that challenged tyranny around the globe. He is also the founder and longtime chair of Human Rights Watch, one of the most respected human rights organizations in the world.

. . .

For fifty years, the banner of Public Affairs Press was carried by its owner Morris B. Schnapper, who published Gandhi, Nasser, Toynbee, Truman, and about 1,500 other authors. In 1983, Schnapper was described by *The Washington Post* as "a redoubtable gadfly." His legacy will endure in the books to come.

Peter Osnos, *Founder*